EUROPE AND THE CHURCH
UNDER INNOCENT III

fact. Heresy was epidemic in parts of Italy and in southern France. On every side the story was the same, faction and strife, disorganization and tumult.

By the same token no Pope ever had a better opportunity to assert his supremacy. An impartial arbiter in Europe was sorely needed. No person was as likely to be above partisan interest and national prejudice as the Bishop of Rome. Surely no person was as unreservedly devoted to the paths of peace. The least sympathetic contemporary would perforce identify with the divine purpose successful intervention in such numerous and such thorny problems. Those already devoted to the papal policies would welcome for them the pragmatic sanction of convenience and success. It was indeed a golden moment for the papacy. Nor could the Pope well dodge the issue. He claimed for himself the apostolic powers of Peter and, in the last analysis, the temporal power of the Roman Emperors. The affairs of Europe were clearly out of joint.

Innocent III was far from shirking either the task or its implications. Stimulated by the widest possible conception of his office he p.oceeded to deal with every question, both great and small, as it confronted him. He threw himself into his work with an energy and a capacity for detail which would have made his name and fortune in any sphere of human activity at any time in the world's history. His extant correspondence, some six thousand letters, reveals his activities over an incredibly wide area. He exerted his influence powerfully in England and in France and ing bands of mercenaries, the residuum of the ill-fated hosts of the late imperial conqueror, Henry VI, swarmed in the central regions. The Sicilian Kingdom, always unmanageable because of its variety of racial stocks and religious faiths, was in the throes of a minority. In the north and west of Europe conditions were hardly more stable. England had already entered the period of feudal reaction and baronial revolt which was to follow the strong rule of Henry II. France, under Philip Augustus, had perfected its monarchical institutions sufficiently to enter upon an aggressive and predatory foreign policy which threatened alike the integrity of the Plantagenet Empire and the peace of Europe. Spain was a maelstrom of feudal principalities milling about towards some as yet rather ill-defined goal, hardly capable of union even in the traditional and vital conflict with the Saracen. In the east the confused rivalries of Magyar and Slav promised anything but peace for themselves or for their neighbors. The Byzantine Empire, so necessary as a bulwark for Europe against Asiatic foes and so important for the near-by Christian states as a cultural center, was visibly tottering to its fall. The Kingdom of Jerusalem, costly product of European crusading efforts for a full century, was but the shadow of the principality set up with such enthusiasm by the First Crusade. The Church itself hardly escaped the prevailing discord. Many bishops submitted to papal guidance in justice, finance, liturgy, or morals with bad grace if at all. Simony was to be found everywhere. Clerical celibacy was a tradition but not a the Pope which Innocent had perfected and at the same time serves as a striking climax to a brilliant pontificate; the latter is a revolutionary document asserting that the papal authority is a delegated authority, actually dependent upon the Church in Council assembled. The papacy weathered the storm, to be sure, but not in the medieval period. In the secular sphere, in its ability to control or direct the states of Europe in matters not strictly ecclesiastical, whether by holding the balance of power among them, through the appellate jurisdiction of its court, or by the frank use of ecclesiastical censures for political purposes, the papacy has never returned to the status established by Innocent III.

The explanation of this remarkable ascendancy of the Bishop of Rome both in Europe and in the Church during the relatively brief period of the pontificate of Innocent III is to be found partly in the conditions which prevailed both in Europe and in the Church at his accession, partly in the traditions already clustered about the papal throne, and to a very considerable extent in the personality and driving force of its occupant during those eighteen years.

No Pope in the medieval period ever found Europe more hopelessly divided and confused than did Innocent III, nor the Church more ready for direction and leadership. The imperial crown was in dispute and the Empire filled with resultant warfare and anarchy. Italy was immersed in a sea of troubles. In the north of the peninsula the interminable conflict of city against city was in full swing. German adventurers and rov-

EUROPE AND THE CHURCH UNDER INNOCENT III

INTRODUCTION

The medieval papacy attained the flood tide of its power in the pontificate of Innocent III. At no other time have its achievements in both ecclesiastical and secular affairs so nearly coincided with its claims to world-wide competency. Innocent III promulgated openly and persistently the same sweeping theories of papal prerogative in Church and in State which his predecessors had hardly dared to commit to writing even in their private papers. Europe listened to him; frequently it obeyed him. Yet only a century later one of his successors, Boniface VIII, suffered ignominious defeat in a great struggle with Philip IV of France. His words were the words of Innocent but they were entirely devoid of any substance of power. The ebbing tide of papal strength displays itself even more forcibly in the great reforming Councils of the fifteenth century since they attacked papal supremacy in the Church itself. It is a far cry from the Fourth Lateran Council of 1215 to the decree *Sacrosancta* of the Council of Constance in 1415. The former ratifies the monarchical organization of the Church under

CONTENTS

PREFACE

This account of Europe and the Church under Innocent III is neither a biography of Innocent III nor a history of Europe during his pontificate. It is an attempt to explain, in reasonably brief ·compass, why Innocent III has long been recognized as the greatest of the medieval popes, and to suggest the extent to which this characterization is justified. Based for the most part on the magisterial studies of Achille Luchaire (*Innocent III,* 6 vols., Paris, 1904-1908), this small volume presents to the general reader, it is hoped, enough detail concerning the multifarious and complicated activities of Pope Innocent III, both secular and ecclesiastical, to give a clear understanding of his career and its significance for both Europe and the Church. The culmination of his pontificate, the Fourth Lateran Council in 1215, twelfth among the great ecumenical councils of the Western Church, will be of special interest for mid-twentieth-century readers familiar with the twenty-first and latest in the series, Vatican II, in Rome from 1962 to 1965.

The table of contents has been somewhat condensed and a supplementary paragraph has been added to the bibliographical note: otherwise the book stands as originally published in 1927.

S. R. P.
1968

EUROPE AND THE CHURCH
UNDER INNOCENT III

BY

SIDNEY R. PACKARD

PROFESSOR OF HISTORY, EMERITUS, SMITH COLLEGE

NEW YORK / RUSSELL & RUSSELL

in Spain. The Empire and Italy were always his particular concern. He had a large program in the east of Europe. He turned the Fourth Crusade to his purpose though he could not control it. He made an heroic effort to unite the Eastern and Western Churches. He treated the monarchs of Europe as his sons and, though an indulgent father, he did not spare the rod. Yet he never forgot his duties as head of the Church. He was keenly interested in its liturgy, in the morals and the education of its clergy, and in its financial and judicial organization. A jurist himself, he drew heavily upon collections of canons recently made by partisans of the papal cause, collections which were veritable arsenals of documents suited to his purpose. His own court was a court of first and last resort for all Christendom; through it he came into contact with almost every contemporaneous question. No matter was too small to attract his attention or too mighty for his ambition. The Fourth Lateran Council of 1215, one of the really great Councils of medieval Europe, is justly indicative of the interests and achievements of Innocent III in strictly ecclesiastical matters as well as in those tinged or suffused with political significance.

But it must be remembered that Innocent III stood squarely on the shoulders of other men. The succession to which he belonged antedated all the royal families of Europe, could not be exposed to the dangers of a minority, and rarely even went through the forms of a regency. Leo I and Gregory I were his predecessors and had long since accustomed men to a papacy which was European in scope and divine in sanction. By the middle of the eleventh century the Pseudo-Isidorian Decretals had given to the Pope superiority over the bishops; the Cluniac reform in the same century had marked out the *terrain* for the inevitable conflict of Church and State. In that conflict the question of lay investiture of ecclesiastical officers is writ large, but the willingness and ability of the papacy to deal with the sovereigns of Europe as its subordinates is writ even more indelibly. Canossa entered rapidly into the European mind and with it a realization of papal leadership, personified by Gregory VII. Even the Concordat of Worms, compromise though it was between the mutually conflicting and legitimate interests of Church and State, added prestige to the papacy which could force it upon the secular rulers as a working agreement.

The protracted struggle between Popes and Hohenstauffens in the twelfth century strengthened the hand of the Pope even more. Frederick Barbarossa might glory in the paper victory at Constance over the recalcitrant Italian towns and dazzle friend and foe alike with the resplendent pageantry of that feudal field-day at Mainz in 1184, but the truce of Venice which preceded had advertised the humiliation of the Empire at the hands of Pope Alexander III before the most brilliant diplomatic congress Europe had yet seen. Moreover, Italy and the Guelf nobles of Germany had found a defender of their interests against imperial power. It may well have been that they loved the Emperor less rather than the Pope more,

but they stood in sore need of the latter as the son of
Frederick Barbarossa, Henry VI, prepared to push the
plans of his father to a more successful conclusion,
with the aid of his Sicilian acquisitions by marriage.
His sudden death relieved the tension, though only
momentarily, for the imperial menace was inherent in
the imperial office and not a thing to disappear with
the death of any individual. The Popes found themselves, perhaps to their own surprise, the champions
of various and conflicting factions allied only in their
opposition to established secular authority, but they
were unmistakably the champions of these forces.
Concurrently a great institution, Monasticism, and a
great movement, the Crusades, had combined to make
effective papal control of Europe in both town and
parish and papal leadership in the popular imagination
as well as in actual fact.

As a result the older theories of papal prerogative
were confirmed and new theories produced. To Innocent III we owe not only their sharpest definition
but also what may be described as their classical
presentation. The Donation of Constantine, by which
the Emperor was alleged to have abdicated his authority in Italy (it was afterwards said in the whole Western Empire), had long since been established as a
basis for papal prerogative in secular affairs. Innocent
III went beyond this and by an assertion of a translation of power from east to west at the coronation
of Charlemagne claimed for himself and his successors
the full *imperium* of ancient Rome. Not only must
an Emperor-elect rely upon papal confirmation but

the Empire reverted to the papacy when vacant and the Popes were the sole arbiters in disputed elections. This theory entered the canons of the Church through the decretals of Gregory IX, thus achieving relative permanence however tenuous its strictly historical accuracy may seem to modern criticism.

The superiority of the spiritual over the temporal power had likewise long been an accepted idea and Europe was familiar with the symbols of the two swords, the soul and the body, time and eternity, and others of a similar nature. Innocent III reiterated the general thesis many times. "To princes is given earthly power, but to priests power in heaven. The former rule our bodies, the latter our souls. The power of the priest surpasses that of the prince to the same degree that the soul transcends the body." Indeed no one doubted the existence of these two spheres of authority nor the supremacy of the spiritual officer. Innocent III, however, contributed a new metaphor. "As God placed two great lights in the starry heavens, a greater light to preside by day and a lesser to preside by night, so he established in the realm of the Universal Church two great powers, one to rule the souls of men and one to rule their bodies. As the moon, inferior in size and quality, draws its light from the sun, so the royal power derives its splendor from the priestly." As for himself, Innocent III stated frankly that he was above men and below God, the very Vicar of Christ.

All this seemed regular enough to men of the medieval world, accustomed as they were to feudal relationships in a feudal hierarchy of ranks. The concept of

a State apart from the Church was unthinkable.
Neither Pope nor Church claimed direct control of
secular affairs, merely preëminence, i.e., ultimate dominion, usually of importance only in time of dispute
or weakness. Nothing could seem more natural than
a supreme head for the Church, himself the spiritual
overlord of all men and specifically of the princes of
this world who were in their own turn supreme in the
secular sphere. The wide divergence between the
ideal on the one hand and the spotted actuality of discord and quarrel between secular and ecclesiastical
officers on the other did not invalidate the claims of
the Church nor impair the alluring analogies of sun
and moon or of body and soul, so dear to the medieval
habit of thought. The Church continued to assert its
position in season and out. Time fought in its favor.
Defeat for the Emperor in the long struggle of Emperor with Pope was always disastrous, a serious impairment of his prestige and authority. Defeat for the
Church was a momentary setback, one more sorrow
visited upon the man of God who was its leader.
Then too, the Pope was usually allied with the common interest against special classes. As an unrelenting
advocate of peace in a period of feudal anarchy, he
was always the hope of the mass of men.

The medieval concept of a World-State and a
World-Church, working harmoniously in their respective spheres, was an alluring solution for the
governmental ills of the European Commonwealth. It
suggests the idea of a World Court or of a League of
Nations, though there are many and striking differences. That the papacy should lead the Church and

supervise the State seemed perfectly natural; that the papal court should serve as a clearing house for all disputes and, upon occasion, as a World-Tribunal seemed perfectly logical. The papacy was not the product of credulous superstition and fabricated documents but the result of historic growth. It corresponded to real needs in human affairs. It could, and to a very large degree it did under Innocent III, concentrate the moral forces of Christendom against feudal anarchy, warfare, injustice, and human passions. "Though I cannot judge of the right to a fief," he said, "yet it is in my province to judge when sin is committed and it is my duty to prevent all public scandal."

Indeed the modern student will be amazed to discover how nearly Innocent III succeeded in realizing the utopian ideal of a world-organization based upon peace and justice and backed by adequate force, whether spiritual or physical. His failure, patent in the narrative which follows, and the failure of the Church subsequently to make effective the potentialities in this direction which he revealed may well be taken as indications that the scheme itself was wellnigh impossible. A supreme arbiter of the world's affairs pre-supposes a lofty unconcern with immediate or eventual material gain together with a complete devotion to justice and right which one is as unlikely to find in any human agent as the omniscient intelligence which is equally mandatory. The fact that Innocent III failed is not nearly as significant as the degree of success he achieved in the pursuit of an ideal which was itself nothing less than perfection.

No explanation of the accomplishments of the

papacy under Innocent III can possibly evade the fact of his own personality. Offices are but empty things without their incumbents and the See of Peter, a partly human institution by any theory, is no exception. The factors already sketched produced a unique opportunity for the wearer of the triple crown but it would have been useless in the hands of a man unable or unwilling to exploit it.

Lothario of Segni, better known as Innocent III, was born in 1160 or 1161 in Anagni or near-by, not far to the south and east of Rome. His father belonged to a noble family descended from the Lombard Dukes of Spoleto; his patrimony was a county of the Roman Campagna which later gave to the family its name of Conti. Lothario's mother was a daughter of a Roman senatorial house.

Of his youth we know exceedingly little. He received his early education at Rome, then studied theology at Paris and law at Bologna. Paris, of course, was the place above all others where one studied theology and the new scholastic philosophy which Abélard and his followers had popularized. Lothario of Segni was merely one of the hordes of students attracted by this tradition, a Master of Arts at Paris before there was a university. Later in life he frequently displayed that fondness for France and things French which has invariably characterized those privileged with similar student memories. To many of his teachers he gave high ecclesiastical office. Bologna was equally preëminent in the teaching of law, both Civil and Canon. The papal letters of Lothario exude familiarity both with the Corpus Juris Civilis of the great Justinian, so recently revived as an object of study, and with the Decretum, a familiarity which could have been derived at that time only at Bologna and from teachers steeped in the tradition of Irnerius and Gratian. No Frederick Barbarossa or Philip Augustus or Henry II was ever more legally minded than Innocent III nor more successful in packing his councils with men trained in both laws. The organizing and centralizing tendencies of the Roman Law entered even more forcibly into the Church under Innocent III than ever before.

Upon his return to Rome, possessed of the best education then available in Europe, the young Lothario entered immediately upon that career in the Church to which his education and his family connections alike impelled him. Three of his relatives were cardinals; one of them became Pope Clement III in 1187. Thus Lothario became first a Canon of St. Peter's and later, in 1190 and at the age of 29, a cardinal. During the remainder of Clement's pontificate, as might be expected, he was one of the most trusted of papal advisers, gaining an extensive knowledge of the practical details of ecclesiastical organization and government.

The succeeding pontificate, that of Celestine III, was for Lothario a period of forced retirement from active affairs. It is in this interval, a veritable prelude to his real career, that he wrote the most important of the extant treatises from his pen. These writings are informing as to the mentality and predilections of the coming Pope, though the modern student would doubtless consider it cruel and unusual punishment

were he compelled to read them, even in translation.
One was entitled "De contemptu mundi" and was
typically medieval in title, manner, and content.
Scholastic in its accumulation of texts from Holy Writ
and the writings of the Fathers and in its careful
omission of almost every indication of the real thought
of the author, the treatise appears to be the last word
in medieval asceticism. It is one long outpouring of
the physical and moral ills and weaknesses of humanity, accompanied by a brief but vivid account of
punishments, human and divine, alike inevitable. But
the preface states that the author would as willingly
develop the contrary thesis of the grandeur of the
human status. We are obliged to agree with Luchaire,
the learned French biographer of Innocent III, that
the treatise is merely a scholar's exercise, a display
of technique. It reveals his abilities, not his opinions.
The other writings are similarly shot through with the
scholastic theology, garnished with that wealth of
allegory and symbol which the medieval reader so
much admired. One of them, a discussion of the
Mass, is an important source of information concerning that ceremony in his day. By these writings his
world was much impressed, a more important fact
than the modern verdict that they are empty and
academic. These compositions do not reveal an ascetic
nor a mystic, but a man of skill in scholastic argumen-
tation, able to marshal citations for his purpose as
the modern politician uses statistics, and exceedingly
apt in the selection of symbol and allegory in the most
approved medieval style.

Celestine III died on the eighth of January, 1198. Like many another dying monarch he had attempted the impossible, to control the election of his successor. The cardinals, as usual, were much too wary to countenance any such diminution of their power. They assembled the very day of Celestine's death in a fortress between the Circus Maximus and the Coliseum, in the very midst of ancient Rome. The first ballot gave a clear majority to Lothario of Segni and, with some misgivings because of his youth (he was then only 37), the vote was made unanimous. The cardinals did homage to their new chief, conferred the name of Innocent upon him in token of his blameless life, and announced their choice to the waiting populace.

Crowds of citizens immediately thronged about the new Pope, escorted him to the basilica of St. John Lateran, and witnessed there his formal enthronement. Six weeks later he was consecrated as Pope in the basilica of St. Peter with all the pomp and ceremony which the church could muster. The tiara, with its implications of political domination over Church and people, was substituted for the episcopal mitre upon his head and the new Pope took his place in a triumphal procession which wound a tortuous way from the new Rome beyond the Tiber through the old to the papal palace adjoining St. John Lateran. Innocent III, as he forced his way through cheering crowds to the papal residence, must have felt like a Roman Emperor at the height of his career. Upon his arrival the pontificate of Innocent III may be said to have begun.

What was the attitude of this successor of St. Peter toward the dignity which he had just assumed? When elected he had at first refused, a traditional gesture among Popes-elect. His inaugural sermon and the letters by which he notified the princes of Europe of his accession, notably that to Philip Augustus, tell a different story. There is in them a decent yet exaggerated humility, but there is also a consciousness of power. It may well have been the power of God working through humble and human hands, but it is unmistakably power. "Who am I and of what lineage that I should take my place above Kings? For to me it is said in the Prophets, 'I have this day set thee over nations and over the kingdoms, to root out and pull down, and to destroy, and to throw down, to build and to plant.' To me it is said in the Apostles, 'I will give unto thee the keys of the kingdom of heaven; and whatsoever thou shalt bind on earth shall be bound in heaven: and whatsoever thou shalt loose on earth shall be loosed in heaven.' The successor of Peter is the Vicar of Christ: he has been established as a mediator between God and man, below God but beyond man; less than God but more than man; who shall judge all and be judged by no one."

The specific deductions which may be made from these premises do not greatly matter nor is it of much use to scrutinize the logic with which they are drawn or the historical accuracy of the facts involved. The whole philosophy of Innocent III is here, patent and without pretense. He conceived himself to be God's representative upon earth, competent to do His will in human affairs.

CHAPTER I

ITALY AND THE EMPIRE

The initial problem of the pontificate of Innocent III, as of every Pope in the medieval period, was the city of Rome. He would seem a weak man indeed who could not be master of his own episcopal city, but examples were not wanting of Popes who could rule the world but not Rome. For Rome was a commune in the twelfth century like Milan or any other Italian town, reeking with democratic enthusiasm and aristocratic pride, defiant of overlords, episcopal and imperial alike. In addition it was an historic city, the center of a great Republic and Empire which had once held the world in fee. The old city surrounding the Capitol was a graphic reminder of glory that had waned. The least provocation turned men's thoughts back to traditions of independence and power. The Leonine city, centered upon St. Peter's and the Vatican and protected against the old by Hadrian's mausoleum, the fortress of St. Angelo in medieval times, seemed to the Romans an excrescence, a thorn in the side of the Roman body politic. The threefold character of the Pope as Bishop of Rome, head of the Church, and temporal ruler left them cold. To them he was only an episcopal overlord; his wider pretensions merely served to alarm them for the safety of the commune and to revive memories of their own ancient splendor.

On that February day in 1198 when Innocent III traversed the city as a newly consecrated Pope, he was accompanied by the Prefect, an appointee of the late Emperor and sole representative of imperial power in Rome, by the Senator who was for the moment in charge of the municipal government produced by the mid-twelfth century communal revolution so closely associated with the fiery Arnold of Brescia, and by the nobles of the district, both urban and provincial. On that same day the Prefect tendered an oath of submission. His imperial master was dead and the Empire in abeyance; he could well afford to exchange devotion to the Pope for protection by him. With the commune Innocent III was equally prompt. He recognized it as his immediate predecessors had done, but he forced the selection of officials who would not oppose his plans.

Actually, this made little difference. The commune conducted its affairs at the Capitol in utter disregard of papal interests, much as before. In 1199 it even made war against Viterbo, a papal town. Innocent III prayed publicly for the Roman armies and acquiesced in their victory over his own dependents, apparently hoping to salvage peace and Roman gratitude from a situation which promised no other advantages.

The great noble families of the Roman district, the Pierleoni, the Frangipangi, the Colonna, the Orsini, and the Conti themselves, each with a fortified stronghold in the city, constituted an additional difficulty. Their protracted and virulent rivalries drove Innocent III into virtual exile at Anagni in 1203. The commune induced him to return in 1204, but the feuds continued.

The intransigent spirit of the commune, always smoldering, flared up seriously for the last time in 1208, and then briefly. Gradually the city came to realize that it depended in the long run upon the Pope. The Rome of 1200 boasted hardly more than thirty-five thousand souls. To it came churchmen and pilgrims in increasing numbers. They required food and lodging. Many stayed months and even years. Usually they borrowed extensively before their departure. Thus there seemed to be good reasons both for papal residence in the city and for free communication between it and the outside world. Moreover, the Pope was generous to the city in the old Roman way. There was a general distribution of silver upon his consecration day and at frequent intervals thereafter, notably in the famine year of 1202. In 1204 Innocent III founded a hospital, later and still known as the hospital of the Holy Spirit, which ministered to the Romans, man, woman, and child, saint or sinner, itself a pioneer among such municipal institutions and avowedly a model for the rest of Europe.

A full decade had elapsed before Innocent III and Rome evolved a working arrangement which was mutually satisfactory, but the last eight years of his pontificate were comparatively peaceful. Even the Roman mob hesitated before the master of half the world.

CENTRAL ITALY

The territorial possessions of the Popes in central Italy, the Patrimony of Peter, had the vaguest of boundaries and within them the papal rights were still less sharply defined. The Donations of the Carolingians and the tacit or expressed confirmations by many of their successors, together with the legacy of the Countess Matilda, had accustomed the papacy to the idea of sovereignty in the region about Rome and in the old Exarchate of Ravenna, the whole comprising a diagonal strip across the peninsula from Ravenna to the northern boundary of the Neapolitan Kingdom.

No authority in the Middle Ages could exist, whether temporal or spiritual, without a considerable territorial basis. In founding the States of the Church the Popes were acting in accord with medieval common sense and established political experience. Within the limits of the Patrimony, however, they played much the same rôle as the Capetian King in France. They were suzerains in theory, only occasionally in fact. Unlike the Capetians, unfortunately, their principal opponents were towns and the communal spirit, not nobles and feudalism. In addition, they lacked the Capetian armed forces.

This weakness of the Popes became almost fatal in the latter part of the twelfth century due to the encircling ring of their enemies. The Lombard towns in the north, to be sure, were virtually independent and the Sicilian Kingdom in the south was a papal fief, but imperial troops were established in Tuscany, advance guards, as it were, of imperial forces which would swallow up Italy itself.

Frederick Barbarossa had revived the regalian rights of the Roman Emperors over the Italian towns, papal as well as others, and, although the results had hardly been satisfactory for Frederick, they proved scarcely less disastrous both for Italian unity and for papal control of Italy. Henry VI, whose death preceded the accession of Innocent III by only four months, had perfected extensive plans for the development of imperial ambitions. He meant to conquer Italy, to incorporate it into the Empire along with the Sicilian Kingdom which he had acquired by marriage, and to proceed then to the control of the Mediterranean, possibly attacking Constantinople itself. In the back of his mind lurked a scheme to make the imperial crown, thus glorified, hereditary in the house of Hohenstauffen.

All this boded ill for the papacy. Nor were the specific results of the Hohenstauffen advance reassuring. Henry VI poured German troops into Italy in large numbers, together with a small army of German officials, carved up the imperial conquests in central Italy into suitable fiefs, and gave them to German barons. His brother, Philip of Suabia, was made Duke of Tuscany. Markwald of Anweiler became Margrave of Ancona and Duke of Ravenna. Conrad of Herslingen became Duke of Spoleto. The imperial conquest of Italy, so frequently threatened and so long delayed, seemed only a matter of persistence.

The untimely death of the Emperor put an abrupt

end to these grandiose schemes on the very eve of their accomplishment. Innocent III, at the moment of his accession, saw his chance and "entered the Empire through the grave of Henry VI." In Italy this meant the championship of the Italian cities against the German invaders plus the strengthening of the papal lordship within the Patrimony at every possible point and in every conceivable way. The oppressive tactics of the German leaders and the brutal excesses of the German soldiery had so aroused the anger of Italians as to make the task easier. For the moment papal and communal policies in Italy coincided.

Markwald of Anweiler, ruler of Ancona and Ravenna, and Conrad of Spoleto both attempted to buy an alliance with Innocent III in view of the altered conditions in the peninsula, promising the most alluring territorial acquisitions, but Innocent III clung fast to the hatred of the German invaders which was his principal weapon. He borrowed money, raised troops, excommunicated Markwald and Conrad, absolved their subjects from allegiance, and drove them out of Italy. In the Exarchate the Archbishop of Ravenna gained rather more than the Pope as a result of these events but Innocent's conquests in the duchy of Spoleto were extensive. In the summer of 1198 he made a triumphal tour through its cities; even Perugia, for the first time, did homage to a Pope.

In Tuscany the story was somewhat different. Initial successes awakened hopes that the papacy might regain the whole of this prosperous region; actually it recaptured only the old cities of the Patrimony in this region which had been wrested from the Church by Henry VI. Florence, Lucca, and Siena preserved their independence. Pisa remained Ghibelline. Innocent III placed new officials in the reconquered cities, erected fortresses, and strengthened his northern boundary.

Within the papal Patrimony, thus enlarged and restored, Innocent III had his troubles. It was the misfortune of the papacy that the communal spirit and the lay spirit combined against it except in the moments of direst need. It was to the cities of the Papal States that Innocent III addressed that remarkable letter in which he develops the metaphor of sun and moon as symbols of spiritual and secular power. At Viterbo, in 1207, he held a kind of estates-general of the Patrimony, to which bishops, abbots, counts, barons, podestàs, consuls, and other officials were summoned. In it he promulgated two principles, the superiority of the spiritual over the temporal power and the police power of the papacy within the Papal States. But the promulgation of law and the enforcement of it were two quite different things in the thirteenth century as in the twentieth. It may have been true that Innocent III possessed the rights of an Emperor in central Italy, but he certainly lacked his army. Ecclesiastical censures have never proved very satisfactory substitutes for armed force in matters of government; Innocent III discovered that they became less effective with each succeeding year.

The full significance of Innocent's activities in central Italy, however, is not greatly impaired by defects in governmental machinery which, after all, were common to every thirteenth-century state. The major fact emerges that an energetic Pope had established the States of the Church upon what proved to be a relatively permanent footing, not only within a few months of apparent total eclipse by imperial forces but in the very first year of his own pontificate. The effect of such an achievement upon European public opinion and upon Italian loyalties may not be calculable but it must be reckoned with; the effect upon the character and subsequent career of Innocent III himself was undoubtedly even more important.

THE KINGDOM OF THE TWO SICILIES

The Norman Kingdom in southern Italy, including also Sicily and Malta, was both a great danger and a unique opportunity for Innocent III. Founded by Norman adventurers in the eleventh century just as the resurgent papacy was carrying its reform program and its temporal ambitions to the culmination at Canossa, it was a very real obstacle in the path of eventual papal domination in the peninsula and at the same time a protection for the Popes against the Greek, Saracen, and Italian elements of which it was composed. The former consideration had seemed more vital to the Popes from the first, but they had been defeated in the initial trial of strength with the Norman leaders. The latter, freebooters and brigands without place or party in feudal Europe, had been quite content to exchange feudal homage to the Pope

for formal recognition by him as Dukes of Calabria
and Apulia and of Sicily.

The feudal bond, however, was a tenuous one and
the Norman Kingdom came to be a vigorous state.
This is not the place to describe its unique features,
the curious blending of Norman strong central government with Byzantine bureaucracy, its tolerance of
such varied religious groups as the Saracen, Greek
Orthodox, Jewish, and Christian, or its enormous material resources based upon maritime preëminence,
thriving towns, and a rich agricultural hinterland. To
many it appears by the mid-thirteenth century as the
prototype of the modern State; even those most impressed by its weaknesses and its ephemeral life remain
to praise its brilliance and to marvel at its precocious-
ness in the short interval of its existence from 1059
to 1250.

The papacy had no right to the southern Kingdom
save the legendary Donation of Constantine and the
voluntary action of the Norman ruler in 1059. The
marriage of the future Henry VI of the house of
Hohenstauffen to Constance, heir-presumptive of the
reigning King of Sicily, in 1186, must have aroused
grave doubts in many minds concerning the permanent
peace in Italy which it was supposed to guarantee; as
events turned out, it displayed the full potentialities
of the Norman lands.

William II of Sicily died in 1189, leaving Henry
heir to the Sicilian crown. There was opposition in
Sicily against a German master, effective in 1191, in-
effective in 1194. In the latter year, Henry VI, now

Emperor, gained complete mastery of the Kingdom, placed Germans in high office, and entrusted the government to Constance, his wife, whose Norman blood and Norman sentiment would ensure the success of an indubitably foreign rule.

By this virtual incorporation of the Sicilian Kingdom into the Empire the plans of Henry VI forged ahead. Hohenstauffen power was paramount at both ends of the peninsula and was being progressively tightened in the center. In 1194 Constance gave birth to a son, the future Frederick II. Thus Henry VI not only looked forward to using his Italian conquests as a stepping-stone for Mediterranean exploits which would revive the most glorious days of Justinian, but he also was able to contemplate the very difficult step of making the imperial crown hereditary in his house.

The Pope of the period, Celestine III, opposed this dangerous aggrandizement of the Hohenstauffen as best he could. He stressed the fact that Sicily was a papal fief; he reiterated that Henry lacked any legal title to the lands just granted out to German chieftains in central Italy. Innocent III said later that Celestine III refused the invitation to grant the whole Empire to Henry as a fief in exchange for confirmation of imperial control in Italy and of the hereditary principle. Certain it was that an hereditary ruler of Italy would have been of little use to the papacy, vassal or no. Certain it was also that, by 1196, imperial control in the south had added practically the final touch to the imperialization of Italy, leaving the papacy isolated and impotent.

Henry VI, a remarkable man by any count, died suddenly in 1197, at the age of thirty-three. In comparison with his father who was the medieval ideal of warrior and knight, he was an unlovely figure. Cruel and vindictive, yet energetic and far-sighted, he was the least attractive of the medieval Emperors and the one who came nearest to the attainment of universal Empire and world-wide dominion. It is not possible to estimate the extent to which his example influenced Innocent III and induced him to think in imperial terms, but it is perfectly clear that the death of Henry VI gave the new Pope, four months later, his great opportunity, not only in Italy and in Germany, but especially in the southern Kingdom.

In 1198, when Innocent III became Pope, Sicily was under a Regent acting for a three-year-old child. The Regent herself was anti-German in her sympathies; the bulk of the population was ardently so. Memories of German cruelty and the presence of German officials and troops made the moment an auspicious one for the assertion of papal sovereignty in the clearest fashion.

Innocent III first ensnared Constance into the reception of a bull proclaiming papal suzerainty over Sicily. More than that, he forced her to seal a concordat for herself and her son which abolished the ecclesiastical independence earlier enjoyed by the Norman Kings and placed the Sicilian Church upon the same footing as the rest of Christendom in regard to episcopal elections, the holding of councils, and the authority of papal legates. At the same time Constance, seriously ill, entrusted by testament to their papal overlord both her son and her Kingdom. Upon her death, within the year, Innocent sent two legates to take charge of his young ward and to administer the realm. His letter to the youthful Frederick contains the same lofty conception of the papal office which ran through his every utterance; even a contemporary must have seen that fortune had delivered the southern Kingdom into papal hands.

Not until 1208, however, was papal control of Sicily secure. Up to that time German officialdom and feudal opposition to alien rule continued an unequal struggle against ecclesiastical government, aided considerably by that same Markwald of Anweiler whom Innocent had earlier evicted from central Italy. In 1209 Frederick was joined in marriage with Constance of Aragon, widow of a Hungarian King, a match arranged by Innocent III and designed to protect his interests.

There were differences, of course, between Innocent III and his ward, more numerous as Frederick grew older, but mainly concerned with the appointment of royal advisers and with episcopal elections. In the end Innocent III made Frederick Emperor and aided him in gaining possession of his German inheritance. Needless to say, this decision was born of desperation and Frederick was bound in advance by every possible promise and concession in order that the resurrection of the awful specter of the Hohenstauffen might prove as innocuous as possible for the Pope who could find no alternative.

THE EMPIRE

The principal rival of the successor of St. Peter in the Middle Ages was the Emperor. He was the head of the Christian world in secular affairs. He alone could claim on reasonable grounds a political authority comparable in its own sphere with the papal prerogative in matters spiritual. The successors of Charlemagne and of Otto the Great considered themselves the heirs of Caesar Augustus; Henry VI seems to have thought more specifically in the terms of a Justinian. At any rate they claimed no superior save God alone in matters political, though admitting the concurrent authority of the Popes in the ecclesiastical sphere. The Holy Roman Empire may have been literally, as the brilliant phrase of Voltaire would have it, "neither Holy nor Roman nor an Empire," but it was the effective vehicle by which the imperial idea of ancient Rome was transmitted to the modern world. Moreover, it had possibilities as a World-State, at least until the middle of the thirteenth century.

Indeed one explanation of the recurrent and protracted conflict of Pope and Emperor was the fear that the latter might make good in some measure his theoretical right to rule the world, or at least the German and Italian portions of it. The Popes had their own explanation of the coronations of Charlemagne and Otto; they pointed with pride to the Donation of Constantine. They deduced from these facts and from others that they were the rulers of the world, temporal authority being delegated to the Emperor whose election they confirmed. In Italy, for obvious reasons, they retained full control in the region adjacent to Rome.

In practice, of course, both Popes and Emperors were content with a working condition which may be described with Lord Bryce as a compromise between a World-State and a World-Church. The Pope was supreme in spiritual affairs, the Emperor in things secular. They were two complementary functions of the same Power. The one was God's Vicar, the other equally so. They coöperated, for each had need of the other. The coronation of the Emperor by the Pope gave the latter a necessary protection and bestowed upon the former an indispensable confirmation.

A working agreement between two such extreme theories presupposed the nicest balance. The personality of a Gregory VII was hardly more upsetting for his day and generation than the genius of a Frederick Barbarossa or a Henry VI in the later period. Difficult questions of feudal adjustment, such as lay investiture of ecclesiastical officers and the control of Italy, not to mention the shifting background of European political development and its growing national states, inimical alike toward Church or State as an all-embracing institution, all made precarious or quite impossible that careful counterpoise which alone promised peace between Pope and Emperor.

If the latter had more to fear in the century of Canossa, the Popes certainly had the greater cause for alarm in the days of the Hohenstauffen. The henchmen of Barbarossa had vehemently repudiated the fancied insinuation by Pope Hadrian IV that the Em-

pire was a papal fief. Excommunications loosed against
Frederick Barbarossa himself had hardly echoed beyond the Alps. Of all the national Churches of the
Middle Ages the German Church was least ultra-
montane, least dependent upon papal support and least
amenable to papal discipline. Frederick Barbarossa
and Henry VI made practically the entire higher clergy
of Germany Hohenstauffen, sold episcopal sees as they
wished, and confiscated revenues of vacant offices.
In a word they appointed the leaders of the Church
in its conflict with the State and appropriated the contents of the ecclesiastical war chest to boot.

Nor could the more distinctly secular plans of the
two Emperors have appeared less vital to the very life
of the Church. Frederick Barbarossa capitalized the
revived interest in Roman law at Bologna and pushed
his claims to the imperial rights of a Caesar in Italy,
attempting to march over the prostrate bodies of the
Italian towns to domination of the peninsula. Henry
VI went further, acquiring Sicily by marriage and central Italy by force of arms. The Mediterranean plans
toward which he was turning at his death and the
scheme for an hereditary Empire were awful portents
for the papacy. A few more years of life for Henry
VI and a few lucky strokes of military fortune, plus
the successor that Frederick II proved to be, might
well have placed the Hohenstauffen Empire upon a
solid foundation as a territorial state.

This was not to be. The death of Henry VI in 1197
gave the papacy an opportunity which was as un-
expected as it was providential. As a result, in those

crucial years of the first half of the thirteenth century
when England and France were hammering out the
national governments and territorial boundaries which
determined their fortunes far down into the modern
period, the Empire was at the mercy of the Popes.
The rest of Europe might come to grips with feudal
anarchy and explode the imperial fiction which mili-
tated against national strength, but not the Empire
where both things were rampant. The greatest Pope
of the Middle Ages chained the Empire to the disorder
of a disputed election for a full decade and then entrusted it, for his own purposes, to a young and semi-
alien prince tied in advance and at every point by
concession and promise to the Roman pontiff. The
successors of Innocent III carved the Sicilian Kingdom out of the Empire and threw it as a plaything to
French, Spanish, and Hungarian adventurers for six
centuries. The remainder of the imperial body politic,
its strength gone and its vitality sapped by three centuries of Italian intrigue and plot, was flung back
across the Alps to be restored in 1273 on a German
basis by a new dynasty, slowly, painfully, hopelessly
inferior to its neighboring states.

In the relations of Innocent III with the Empire the
initial fact is that disputed election which originated
in the year of his accession and ran its course until
1208. Thus the death of Henry VI which had given
Innocent III sufficient elbow room in Italy to enable
him to establish the Papal States and perfect the papal
control of Italy, furnished him even greater opportu-
nities in Germany.

He proceeded to deal with the Hohenstauffen prelates, to extend papal discipline to all parts of the German Church, and to guarantee by every possible device the feudal particularism of Germany against the centralizing and hereditary tendencies of the Hohenstauffens. In all of this it is apparent again and again that although Innocent III expressed papal theories in their most uncompromising form, actually he was influenced by very practical considerations. He was a diplomat. He knew how to match concession with concession, how to give way at one point only to bring more successful pressure at another. After all he was legally minded and trained in the scholastic philosophy. He may not have made the worse appear the better cause, but his letters are persuasive. They reek with authority and citations of authorities from the Bible and from the Fathers, from the Civil law and from the canons. It is not necessary to impute to Innocent III the craft and guile of a Machiavelli, nor is it possible to evaluate motives across seven centuries, but the wily Florentine would certainly have advised the prolongation of the anarchy in Germany to the last possible moment. It is indisputable that these ten years of German and imperial impotence formed the necessary preliminary for Innocent's power and prestige, not only in Germany and in Italy, but throughout Europe as well.

This is not to assert that the disputed election following the death of Henry VI admitted a simple solution. The German princes had sworn allegiance to the infant Frederick in his father's lifetime, but they did not want a boy of three as Emperor nor would that solution have been wise for him or for them. Neither did they wish to surrender the elective principle. Furthermore, they foresaw that Innocent III, consulting his own interests, would not confirm the election of a Hohenstauffen nor that of a person who controlled both Germany and Sicily. Various candidates were suggested, including such contrasting figures as the calculating Capetian Philip and the gallant and debonair Plantagenet Richard. The majority of the German princes, however, favored either Philip of Suabia or Otto of Brunswick.

Philip was a brother of Henry VI and a Hohenstauffen, steeped in the Ghibelline tradition of the last two Emperors, and supported by Philip Augustus of France. Otto was a Guelf, personified baronial opposition to central power, counted on papal aid for himself and his party, and was the favorite of northern Germany and of his uncles, Richard and John, successively Kings of England from 1189 to 1216.

Both men were elected Emperors by their respective factions in the course of 1198 but neither man was in undisputed possession of the Empire. In days which far preceded the relatively stable constitutional machinery of the seven Electors established by the Golden Bull of 1356 it was not easy for any one to know who was actually the Emperor under such conditions. To refer the whole question to the Pope seemed the natural thing to do and it was done by both parties almost immediately.

Innocent III, on the basis of his own conception of

his office, should have decided impartially for one of
the candidates.   Europe undoubtedly expected a
definite word from the Lateran, especially at the outset when such a decision would have counted heavily.
The Pope, however, hesitated. It was true, of course,
that Philip was of the viper brood of the Hohenstauffen, had himself taken a prominent part in the
descent upon Italy under Henry VI, and was at the
moment still under sentence of excommunication for
his excesses against the Church.   Otto, on the other
hand, was weak, both in the number and the importance of his adherents and in the source of his foreign
aid.   Still, the papal responsibility was clear.   The
enemies of the papacy will say with force that Innocent III delayed in order to bargain more effectively
with both sides.

The real difficulty seems to have been that neither
candidate would throw himself at the feet of the Pope
with quite the abandon which he desired and that
neither candidate would grant actual concessions regarding ecclesiastical lands in Italy.   It will be remembered that Innocent III felt the Italian question to
be absolutely vital in 1198 and in 1199 but that he
was very successful in those years in arranging a satisfactory solution, largely due to this disputed election
in the Empire.   At last, after due consideration (or
was it interminable delay?), he decided for Otto and
proclaimed him as Emperor in January, 1201. Philip's
party replied with a blast against papal interference
in imperial elections.   Innocent replied with a reasoned
statement of the papal right to interfere in case of dis-

pute and of his ultimate authority, if need arose, to select any Christian prince as Emperor.

The great bulk of the German higher clergy sided with Philip. The great prelates were Hohenstauffen appointees. Furthermore, they and their immediate subordinates were also territorial princes, keenly apprehensive of trans-Alpine control. They were especially opposed to the interference of Innocent III in the German Church itself. They resented his legates, his control of episcopal elections, and his supervision of appointments to the most minor offices. It was true that Innocent III based his action at every point upon the canons of the Third Lateran Council of 1179, but the German prelates were as much alarmed by his evident purpose to make himself master of the German Church as their predecessors had been when confronted with the reforming program of Gregory VII. To them Innocent's interference in the imperial election seemed all of a piece with his centralizing and domineering tendencies in the Church and they would have none of him or of his works.

The lower clergy, natural opponents of their ecclesiastical superiors, were Guelf and papal, but their contribution to the cause of Otto IV was inconsiderable. The German nobles, it is true, were more often Guelf than Ghibelline, but they were not united. They saw more clearly than did Innocent III the advantages of disunion and chaos. From them one could expect opposition, but not support. Thus until 1208 Germany was prey to civil war.

Otto IV had at his disposal the full resources of the

papal arsenal but the excommunications and interdicts
which were lavished upon his cause proved sorry
weapons for an imperial campaign. The personal
unpopularity of Innocent III in Germany, so strik-
ingly revealed in the contemporaneous songs of Walther
von der Vogelweide, was an additional disadvantage.
Foreign aid did not materialize sufficiently to turn the
balance. As each weary year gave place to its even
more dreary successor the cause of Otto grew weaker
and weaker, though the bloodshed involved doubled
and redoubled. By the end of 1207 every one had had
enough, including Innocent himself.

The Pope prepared for his reversal of sympathy by
lifting the anathema still resting upon Philip and by
receiving from him an oath of fidelity. All was in
readiness for the confirmation of a Hohenstauffen Emperor and the definitive abandonment of Otto. At that
crucial moment, early in 1208, Philip was assassinated,
following a private quarrel. Otto IV, on the eve of
complete eclipse, was undisputed Emperor. Contemporaries, doubtless including Innocent III himself,
considered the event an act of God.

For a few brief months Emperor-elect and Pope were
fast friends. An extraordinarily well-attended Diet at
Frankfort ratified the election of Otto and he proceeded to stabilize his position in Germany by successive Diets at Nuremberg, Brunswick, Wurzberg, and
at Spires, always looking forward to his coronation at
Rome at the hands of his benefactor. His journey
thither over the Brenner and through the Guelf cities
of Italy was a veritable triumphal march. Pope and

Emperor met at Viterbo. Innocent III preferred promises concerning the lands of the Church in Italy prior to the coronation, but did not press the point, whether from lack of heart or from lack of nerve. In late October, 1208, the coronation of a new Caesar took place in the basilica of St. Peter.

From the instant the imperial crown touched his head Otto became as Ghibelline as the haughtiest of the Hohenstauffens and as careless of the rights of the Church. The disgraceful brawls which had broken out upon the eve of the coronation between the German soldiers and the Roman populace were an inauspicious beginning, but worse was to follow. In the four years following his coronation in 1208 Otto resumed control of Tuscany, invested one follower with the Duchy of Spoleto and another with the Principality of Salerno, claimed Apulia as his own, made peace with the Lombard League, and prepared for war against Naples. His ultimate aim seems to have been the combined occupation of Italy and the southern Kingdom, largely at the expense of the Pope, partly at the expense of the Hohenstauffen Frederick. Much less than this would have sufficed to turn Innocent III from ally to foe. He remonstrated with Otto at the outset, then attacked him with every weapon upon which he could lay his hand. He appealed to Philip Augustus for aid, admitting in one of the most curious letters dispatched from Innocent's Chancery that he had been wrong and Philip right in their previously divergent estimates of Otto's character. Innocent threatened the Italian towns with an interdict or with the loss of a university (Bologna), as seemed most appropriate, in an attempt to win them to his side. He wrote to Germany in the most unmeasured terms and in the most violent language to arouse antagonism against Otto. The permanent warfare of priest and medieval Emperor was again in full swing, the more virulent for a brief intermission.

Yet Otto IV, as was the case with almost all the medieval Emperors, forgot that the Empire was essentially a German power. His successes in Italy were encouraging and spectacular but would be of little use if Germany escaped from his control. The German prelates, either dependent upon Innocent III or allied with the Hohenstauffen house, considered the Italian achievements of Otto a dubious asset for the German state. They had heard disturbing tales of Otto's greed and extravagance, coupled with rumors of new and heavy taxation upon the German clergy and sumptuary laws for the regulation of their lives and incomes. All this revived the still small voice of their collective conscience. They concluded that the ills of Germany originated in their broken vows to support the young Frederick. They sent envoys, via Rome, to invite him to assume the imperial crown of his father.

Innocent III must have hesitated a little before taking a step which would classify him as a Ghibelline Pope and raise once more the awful specter of imperial control on both sides of the Papal States, but the ingratitude of Otto and his successes in Italy left the Pope little choice. As things were then going there would soon be no Papal States to defend against the

Emperor or against any one else. After all Innocent III was no more clairvoyant than his contemporaries. He could not foresee the events of the thirteenth century; he doubtless considered the papal peril as great in 1212 as it had been in 1197. Frederick was young and his ward, though one may doubt that Innocent III still retained much faith in the gratitude of princes.

Frederick was now seventeen years of age, married, and a father. His wife objected to the northern project from the first. The Sicilians, fearing that they would become but a province in the reconstituted Empire, warned him of the perfidy of Germans and of the ulterior motives of Innocent III. In later life Frederick would have certainly thought twice before exchanging the sunny shores of the Mediterranean for the cold and dismal region north of the Alps. Sicily, after all, was his home and his native realm. He delighted in its exotic and luxurious products, both natural and political. He never felt at home in the German climate, in its turbulent feudal life, or with its unwritten codes of law.

But all this could hardly be foreseen. In any case a boy of seventeen would not have hesitated long over such an opportunity. Not only did this German invitation hold before him an imperial crown, but through it he could avenge himself upon Otto who had so recently threatened to conquer the southern Kingdom, rehabilitate the glory of his ancestral house, and, doubtless best of all, enter upon a glorious adventure. He was at once Norman, Italian, and German; the blood in his veins was saturated with a blend of bold activity, crafty intrigue, and downright pugnacity. Well-educated in the cosmopolitan Sicilian way and proficient in six languages, his was a restless spirit and an inquiring mind. The qualities which were to astonish Europe in his full manhood and to create one of the most intensely fascinating careers of the Middle Ages, or indeed of all time, would never urge caution under such conditions.

Almost alone and entirely devoid of any military forces, Frederick departed to win an imperial crown. The journey to Rome was comparatively simple and he was well received by the Pope, by the cardinals, and by the municipal authorities. From Rome northwards his progress was more difficult. Genoa was loyal, Milan was not. The passes of Savoy were in the hands of Otto. Frederick dodged from Pavia to Cremona, thence north by practically unused and little known Alpine passes to St. Gall and on to Constance. His arrival at Constance but a few hours before that of Otto and his troops seems to have turned that city to his side and ultimately the whole tide of public opinion in the Rhine valley. The Empire declared in his favor with a unanimity which betrayed German distrust of Otto and accentuated German willingness to trust a foreign and distant prince.

Frederick was elected Emperor at Frankfort in 1213 and later held his court at Ratisbon. Of course he was obliged to bribe the German nobles with various confirmations of their territorial claims and powers both in order to obtain the election and to maintain his position. Probably he could afford to give away what he had never possessed. Otto, whose strength in Italy was almost literally punctured by the turn in German affairs, retired to his Saxon lands in the north. He emerged from this enforced political rustication but once, for the conflict at Bouvines in 1214.

Bouvines has often been called the first modern battle because of its international character and significance. Philip Augustus of France supported Frederick and John of England supported Otto, but there was a good deal more involved than the imperial conflict and the bitter rivalry of Capetian and Plantagenet. Philip was allied with the towns and clergy of France against the great nobles headed by the powerful Count of Flanders. John was in league with the great Guelf princes of the Rhine country and with the Flemish nobles, hoping against hope that the prestige of a victory upon the continent would strengthen his arm against domestic foes. Defeat for Frederick and Philip would not only have evicted Frederick from the Empire; it would very likely have dismembered the rapidly integrating Capetian monarchy. That same defeat would have given Otto a stake in Europe and in the Empire. More than that, it would have prefaced untold projects based upon an Anglo-Flemish-German alliance. But Philip's standards carried the day. The results of Bouvines were the tightening of the hold of Philip Augustus over his recalcitrant nobles and the confirmation of the centralizing tendencies of his house. It sent John to Runnymede to bargain with his barons for his crown. It rescued Frederick from his German foes and forced

Otto into permanent retirement. Finally, an important item, it greatly strengthened the papacy, not only in Europe at large and in France and in England in particular, but specifically in Italy.

Frederick, of course, had seriously weakened his eventual position by concession and promise all along the way. Not only had he yielded much to his German vassals but he had also bound himself hand and foot to his papal overlord. He had recognized the papal suzerainty over the two Sicilies as early as 1212, thus confirming the concession of his mother. He did homage to the Pope in 1213, promised in 1215 to take the cross, and swore, in 1216, that Sicily and the Empire should never be held by the same person. Thus he was obliged to entrust Sicily formally to his son before his own coronation as Emperor. Earlier he had recognized the Papal States, including Ravenna, Spoleto, the lands of Matilda, and other parcels. He acknowledged the right of appeal from the ecclesiastical courts of Norman Sicily to the papal Curia, abandoned the right to enjoy the revenues of vacant ecclesiastical offices, and promised aid to the Church against the heretic throughout his lands. No German Emperor had ever promised so much. Obviously the plans of Frederick Barbarossa and Henry VI for Italy and for the Mediterranean were completely discarded.

Thus the last years of the life of Innocent III were marked by a most unusual phenomenon, an able Emperor and an able Pope at peace one with the other. The modern student enjoys a vantage ground denied to Innocent III and is apt to view somewhat ironically the confidence with which the great pontiff assumed that the peace of Europe was amply assured by the devotion of Frederick II. Innocent III seems not to have realized that he was leaving the Empire to a layman, a German, a Hohenstauffen, and a Sicilian. But it will be noted that Innocent III did control Rome and central Italy at his death and that his successors continued to do so, on the whole, until the sixteenth century brought new dangers from Spain.

Moreover, Innocent III never looked upon the imperial problem as his most important interest and it is, therefore, an inadequate test of his achievements. France, England, his fond project for a crusade, and many other matters, all these things and their countless interactions had to be reckoned with at every turn. It is possible that he never dreamed of dominating the Empire but only of neutralizing its ambitious plans. Perhaps he honestly believed it to be a necessary counterpoise for his own power.

Yet no one can fail to see the enormous advantages for the papacy which the long-drawn-out disputed election in Germany yielded to Innocent III. One has only to compare the situation in Italy under Henry VI or in the days of Otto's headstrong prosperity with the status of 1200 or of 1216 to see the stakes for which Innocent III played and the prize which he won. If the action of Innocent III on the whole European stage depended in any measure upon a papal Rome and upon a Guelf Italy, then his career hinges upon the ten years of strife in Germany and eventually upon the intrepidity and luck of Frederick II. Whether or not

Innocent III created or prolonged the special conditions which reacted so powerfully to his own advantage may well be argued; the dependence of his good fortune as Pope and as temporal ruler of Europe upon a disunited Germany is certainly beyond dispute.

CHAPTER II

INNOCENT III AND THE STATES OF EUROPE

The list of states which admitted themselves to be in some measure dependent upon the papacy during the pontificate of Innocent III, some of them frankly as vassal states, is both long and impressive; it includes, apart from the Empire, England, Aragon, the Two Sicilies, Portugal, Hungary, Poland, Norway, Sweden, Denmark, Bohemia, Bulgaria, Armenia, Jerusalem, and the Latin Empire of Constantinople. It would be tedious to examine the relations of Innocent III with all these states, yet generalizations concerning his policies and even summaries of his achievements fail to carry conviction unless buttressed by a certain amount of specific illustration drawn directly from his contacts with the dominant factors of the Europe of his day. It has seemed most helpful to deal with Spain first, then with France and with England, and finally, and briefly, with the east of Europe.

SPAIN

In the Spanish peninsula, as elsewhere, Innocent III was interested in forcing papal theories upon secular sovereigns, but he considered the perpetual crusade against the Saracen absolutely vital both for Spain and for Europe. Not forgetting the more immediate needs of the ecclesiastical organization, he devoted the greater part of his energies to the imposition of peace upon quarrelsome Christian princes and the utilization of every possible weapon which could contribute to the success of the Reconquest. He had no way of knowing that another Moslem raid from Africa was not imminent, under another Tarik, and necessitating another Tours. Everything hinged upon the success of the crusade, or at least upon its continuance.

Of the five states within the peninsula in 1200, Portugal, Leon, Castile, Aragon, and Navarre, all were products of this crusade. Since the Popes claimed all territory wrested from the infidel and were themselves practically the only source from which a feudal prince might obtain a royal crown, the dependence of these rulers upon the papacy is clear. One is not surprised to find Innocent III using the same magisterial tone with these petty princes which characterized his communications to Otto and to Philip.

Portugal was a vassal state completely submissive to papal policies. Innocent III compelled the rulers of Leon and Castile, by a liberal use of excommunication and interdict, to follow papal instructions. Castile relied upon the Pope in its hour of need for aid and comfort against the long expected onrush of Mohammedan forces from the south. He summoned feudal aid from the other side of the Pyrenees, spurred all Spain to common action, and, in true medieval style, led a solemn procession in the streets of Rome. The resounding victory of Christian Spain on the field of Las

Navas de Tolosa in July, 1212, which followed, seemed a prodigy and a miracle, the evident touch of the divine hand upon western Christendom and upon its energetic leader. Innocent III, before his death, looked upon conditions in Spain more satisfactory both to the Church and to Europe than any his predecessors had ever seen.

The Kings of Aragon had long paid tribute to the papacy but one of their number, Peter II, a contemporary of Innocent III, was a particularly loyal papal vassal. In 1204 this medieval warrior and prince, easy-going and dissolute even by the vague standards of southern France and the adjacent Spanish littoral, journeyed to Rome and afforded Europe an unique spectacle. He swore fealty to the Pope for his Kingdom, deposited a parchment upon St. Peter's altar promising annual tribute, and allowed himself to be crowned by the Pope with the full ceremony of the Church. The thirteenth century did not think in the nationalistic terms dear to the twentieth and many persons undoubtedly considered such an event entirely honorable for the prince concerned, but it was certainly a striking example of the power and prestige of Rome.

FRANCE

Of all the contemporaries of Innocent III perhaps Philip Augustus of France alone was really a foeman worthy of his steel. The son of a pious father and himself a patron of churches and churchmen, the second Capetian Philip was none the less a hard-headed, shrewd politician, completely immersed in the Capetian problem of creating a strong central government out of feudal anarchy and extending the royal domain to include the great feudal holdings, notably those in the hands of the Plantagenet Kings of England. He was a crusader of a sort and appeared to value papal friendship and aid. Yet the independence of his successors is foreshadowed in many of his acts and in his general attitude. He was not much impressed by thunderings from the Lateran nor by threats of excommunication and interdict, nor even by the interdict itself. He did yield to the Pope upon occasion, but not until he had clearly demonstrated that the bulk of the French clergy would stand with the King and not with the Pope in case of dispute; that he yielded at all seems to have been a real proof of Innocent's power and prestige. Philip, however, never gave in to the Pope in the matter of his German policy and he avoided papal excommunication because of his English projects only by the death of the pontiff. It is doubtless of some significance that Innocent III and Philip differed most violently in regard to the personal morals of the latter; Innocent may well have preferred to occupy incontestably ecclesiastical ground in dealing with the only monarch of Europe in his day really in the possession of what the world came to know as royal power.

In 1193 Philip Augustus married as his second wife a Danish princess, Ingeborg, eighteen years of age. It was not a marriage of affection, since Philip had never seen his bride prior to her arrival in France for

the wedding, but a union dictated by political considerations. The King of Denmark, now his brother-in-
law, had vague claims to the English throne dating
from the days of Canute and, more important, a fleet
which would make possible an armed invasion of England. In the midst of the coronation ceremony, on the
day following the wedding, Philip suddenly displayed
the most unmistakable signs of complete dissatisfaction
with Ingeborg. He attempted to send her back to Denmark. The Danes refused to receive her; she herself
refused to go. Philip called a council of barons and
bishops and obtained from them a divorce. Ingeborg
appealed to Rome.

Celestine III sent letters and legates to declare the
divorce of Philip and Ingeborg null and void, all to no
avail. Philip proceeded to marry again, though he was
three times refused as a suitor before being accepted
by the daughter of a Bavarian noble, Agnes of Meran.

Innocent III, at his accession, proceeded to deal with
Philip Augustus with his accustomed energy. His letters took a sharper and sharper tone; his legates received the widest powers. In 1198, since Philip would
neither put away Agnes nor take back Ingeborg, the
interdict was declared upon all territory acknowledging
Philip as ruler. The power of the King was immediately evident in the reaction of the French clergy.
Many of the greatest prelates refused to publish the
interdict at all, others debated its validity. Those who
obeyed it had still to reckon with the King; his
methods were far from gentle.

The interdict was still a powerful weapon in the

year 1198 even though the scrupulous observance of
it which would alone produce its maximum efficiency
was wanting in France. In some parts of the Kingdom
the people did suffer because of it and suffered acutely.
At such a time only two of the sacraments of the
Church were available, baptism and extreme unction.
No burial could take place in consecrated ground. No
church services of any kind were conducted, save at
rare intervals and for the clergy alone, behind closed
doors, with stilled bells and with bated breath. The
multifarious activities of the Church literally ceased,
to the inconvenience of all and to the peril of the
immortal souls of the great body of believers. Less
than a year of these conditions brought even Philip
Augustus to terms.

The whole affair was debated anew and with great
skill at a council held at Soissons in 1201. Philip
brought the discussion to a dramatic conclusion and
avoided the adverse decision which seemed inevitable
by taking Ingeborg behind him on his horse, in full
sight of the council, and galloping off with her as if
she were indeed restored to rank and freedom. He
did not send Agnes of Meran away, however, and
Ingeborg seems to have continued as much a prisoner
as before. Agnes died in 1201 and Philip attempted a
more complete reconciliation with the Pope in the
following year. The latter met him half-way by legiti-
matizing his two sons by Agnes. This concession was
vital for Philip in view of the poor health of his only
son by his first marriage, but it was a rather perilous
precedent for the papacy. Yet in 1203 Ingeborg was

still complaining that she was not treated as wife and
Queen and Innocent was still fulminating in her
behalf.

After the victory over John of England in 1204
Philip was even less tractable. From 1204 to 1211 the
affair dragged on. Neither side quite dared to defy
the other openly; the most that can be said is that both
sides were extraordinarily patient. Not until 1213
was Ingeborg really Queen of France and then her
restoration was not due to the influence of Innocent III
as much as to the recrudescence of the project of an
invasion of England. The invasion did not take place
but Ingeborg retained her position until Philip's death
in 1223 and was honored as Queen-Dowager until her
own death fifteen years later.

The affair of Ingeborg is a curious one. The real
explanation seems to be simply that Philip did not
care for his political bride and, unlike the majority of
his contemporaries under similar conditions, acted ac-
cordingly. It affords, however, a striking illustration of
the relative power of King and Pope. Philip Augustus
defied the papacy for twenty years, despite the fact that
the error was clearly upon his side. In the end he submitted when and as he pleased. Innocent III, on the
other hand, displayed his intriguing proclivities in the
face of equal or superior strength over a long period.
He was willing enough to force the issue in the early
years of his pontificate but as eager to equivocate later
on when affairs in England and in the Empire also hung
in the balance. Still, he persisted throughout in his
original attitude. Not even Philip Augustus could

make the Pope actually abandon his policy. At the same time the zeal which the Pope displayed in keeping the Empire divided and the other states of Europe as vassals of the Holy See may be partly explained by his experience in France. More than one Philip Augustus in Europe would certainly have curtailed papal power very considerably.

Philip Augustus was vitally interested in imperial affairs as his successive alliances with Frederick Barbarossa and Henry VI indicate. He desired aid against England on the one hand and the distraction of the Emperor from the Rhone and Rhine valleys into things Italian or Mediterranean on the other. Hence Otto of Brunswick, nephew of Richard and John of England and closely associated with Cologne and the north and west of Germany, was completely unsatisfactory to Philip Augustus as an Emperor-elect in 1198 for the very same reasons which endeared him to the Pope, surrounded by Hohenstauffen soldiers and stifled by Hohenstauffen ambitions. Philip's contribution to the earlier downfall of Otto was the defeat of John, culminating in the loss of Normandy, Maine and Anjou to France in 1204.

Later, when Innocent III was obliged to turn to Philip of Suabia, the ardor of the French Philip cooled perceptibly. In 1208 Philip Augustus was actively engaged in pushing the alternative candidature of Henry of Brabant. One suspects that Philip Augustus was gaining as much as any one else from a disputed election in Germany and worked as hard to prolong it.

The assassination of Philip of Suabia upset all cal-

culations and put Otto IV upon the imperial throne.
French diplomacy had failed; the union of Otto and
John against France, presumably with the aid of the
Church, seemed only a matter of time. But Otto IV,
once crowned, proved as Ghibelline as any of his
predecessors, just as Philip Augustus himself had pre-
dicted. The best that Innocent III could do was to
raise up Frederick II against Otto and for that project
Philip Augustus contributed support. He helped to
pave the way for the rallying of German forces for
Frederick and furnished the expenses of his election.
Bouvines, in 1214, which sealed the fate of John, Otto,
and Flanders simultaneously and gave Frederick and
Innocent the upper hand in Germany and in Italy, was
the work of Philip Augustus. Surely he was as much
a king-maker as Innocent III himself. The projected
French invasion of England under papal auspices did
not take place but as a plan it is one more example of
the *realpolitik* of Philip Augustus. Innocent III, however, having escaped the clutches of Otto by a narrow
margin, knew better than to allow Philip Augustus to
play the high hand both in the Empire and in England.

In the Albigensian Crusade in southern France which
forms so important a chapter in the history of the
Church and its struggle against heresy, Philip Augustus
took no part. Yet the results of this crusade for him
and for his dynasty were comparable with the fruits of
Bouvines. Innocent's crusading zeal destroyed a
whole civilization which promised much for Europe
even though it was heretical, and with it the baronage
upon which it rested. In the next reign this whole

district became a feudal dependency of the Capetian monarchs.

The relations of Philip Augustus with Innocent III in other matters were not dramatic though they had their moments. Philip ruled his prelates as he did his barons, taxed them, evicted them from their sees, or persuaded them with force to support him against the Pope. He was particularly insistent that the clergy should perform their allotted feudal service, either in person or by proxy; this he enforced despite the interdict and despite numerous appeals to Rome.

At the same time Philip Augustus made every possible effort to tap the heaped-up material resources of the Church and to check or diminish its jurisdiction in matters legal. The royal right to enjoy the revenues of a vacant see or until the confirmation by the King of the bishop-elect, often long delayed, was frequently surrendered by Philip Augustus with all solemnity and almost as frequently exercised. The resultant altercations between King and Pope, or between their subordinates, were intermittent throughout the reign but never assumed the proportions of a major quarrel.

The legalistic character of the French crown, legatee of Justinian through Bologna as well as Innocent III, became clearer with each succeeding year but drew no fire from the latter until the end of his pontificate. In 1204 Innocent III had claimed jurisdiction over the Norman question; this claim Philip vehemently denied. As events turned out Innocent could do nothing and in the end he left the whole matter to the Norman clergy to decide for themselves. Later, after

Bouvines, Philip claimed England as a forfeited fief through his son Louis. Innocent demanded through his legates that it be recognized as a papal fief. He was about to excommunicate both Louis and Philip Augustus when death intervened. Had he lived he would doubtless have seen the French clergy once more supporting the French King against Rome, probably more solidly than before.

France alone among the countries of Europe did not submit to Innocent III in any matter of the first importance. Partly this is because Innocent III never had the leisure to deal with France alone, being always involved in English and imperial problems, in crusades, and in many other things. In major part, however, the comparative independence of France in the face of the world-system of Innocent III was due to its own vitality as a state and to the extraordinary ability of its monarch.

ENGLAND

England occupied a unique position in the medieval world. Because it is farther removed from Rome than the other important states of Europe and separated from the continent by a narrow but frequently tempestuous channel, it has been less thoroughly permeated by the dominant forces in European history. Great movements upon the continent exert their influences upon England at a relatively late date and usually in a somewhat modified form. We should not be surprised that the Britain which was never wholly Roman was also never completely integrated with the medieval ecclesiastical Commonwealth. The Church in England obviously antedates the Church of England by more than a dozen centuries but both are insular in character. Moreover, the Normans in southern Italy and in Sicily whose strongly centralized and (until Frederick II) ecclesiastically independent state was the despair of the papal overlords to whom they found it convenient to do homage, were merely the younger sons of the two-fisted northern giants who conquered England in 1066.

The battle of Hastings was fought under the papal banner as well as under the ducal colors but the Conqueror was hardly decently grateful for its aid. Probably he was right in thinking his success due mainly to Norman cupidity and baronial strong spirits. At any rate, he took an aggressive attitude toward the Popes, even against the great Gregory VII himself. Admittance of papal legates into the Kingdom, appeals from English courts to Rome, elections of bishops and abbots, all were placed and kept under royal control. Two things alone continued to symbolize papal authority in England, Peter's Pence and Monasticism.

The former, an annual, permanent, and compulsory tax of a penny for each hearth in the Kingdom, had been paid by its successive conquerors, partly to avoid papal displeasure, partly to demonstrate, at no great expense, their respect for established custom. Yet in the Middle Ages it was a dangerous thing to pay an annual tax to any one. The medieval world thought in terms of the feudal relationship; one of the usual indications of that relationship, an annual money payment, would inevitably be considered sufficient evidence of the existence of the feudal bond. There were not wanting, on this and on other grounds, those who asserted that England was in fact a papal fief. Gregory VII claimed this relationship vociferously, but in vain. Henry II seems to have admitted it in his day of troubles in 1173, though he repudiated it with sufficient vigor immediately afterwards.

Monasticism also tended to counteract the congenital independence of English ecclesiastical institutions. The great monastic orders were European by nature, not local, and their members were the special wards and the devoted servants of the papacy. In Canterbury, the most important of the English sees since its archbishop was also Primate of all England, the electors were the monks of Christchurch monastery, like their fellows Roman in their sympathies, not English.

Two Kings of England came into contact with Innocent III, the boisterous Richard who was called "Lionheart" and the morose John who scarcely needed his sobriquet of "Lack-land" to distinguish him from either his contemporaries or his descendants.

Richard was an Angevin more than a Norman; by no possible reckoning could he be called English either in birth, nature, or policy. He spent but a few months in England though he reigned for a full decade. A warrior and a knight, he looked upon England merely as a source of supply for his continental life and projects. His prerogative in ecclesiastical matters made possible the taxation of the clergy and the sale of ecclesiastical offices; both were remunerative, though they were illegal and brought him into conflict with the papacy. With Innocent III Richard was not much impressed. He even offered him advice, needless to say quite gratuitously. Innocent replied as an indulgent father to a wayward son in letters filled with rhetoric and symbol, often in ironical imitation of Richard's own epistles.

The main interest of Richard was in Normandy. He was a better soldier than his father or his brother, or, more important, than Philip Augustus. Filled with new ideas in military engineering which he had derived from a varied experience in Palestine and elsewhere, he seized the hill which overlooks Les Andelys on the border of his Norman territory and crowned it with the bold fortress known as Château Gaillard, whose ruins are still reflected in the flowing Seine. A master-stroke, it effectively checked the Norman raids of Philip Augustus. The fact that the hill upon which the castle stood was a part of a manor belonging to the Archbishop of Rouen doubtless made the adventure the more attractive to Richard.

John became King of England in 1199 and for fourteen years carried on a conflict with the Church at home and abroad which can only be characterized as stubborn, virulent, and brutal. It made no difference to him that the Pope was Innocent III or that the Church was at the moment unusually well-organized and enormously wealthy. Little did he care that he was also involved with the French Philip in a fight to the finish for the English lands in France, or that he was at the same time waging the uncompromising war of centralized monarchy against chartered feudal anarchy. In the end his enemies were too much for him. Petulant and over-ambitious but notably lacking any flair for success, he was obliged to surrender his Kingdom to the Pope, receive it back as a papal fief, allow his authority to be exercised through the intermediary of a legate, and leave at his death a papal legate as the guardian of his son and the real Regent of the realm. Though John was a son of the greatest of the Plantagenets it is in his reign that the Plantagenet Empire disintegrates, geographically with the loss of the Norman and adjacent lands, intrinsically with the colossal catastrophe for the crown at Runnymede which the Great Charter codifies.

The last three years of John's life, filled with supine surrender to ecclesiastical and feudal enemies, seem to have blinded posterity to the long conflict which preceded. Similarly, his failures in Normandy, at Bouvines, at Runnymede, and before the Pope, have persuaded most historians that he was a mean man, of little vigor, military or otherwise, a weakling on every count.

It is true that John's personal life seems to justify the darkest picture of his character and ability, though we must remember that Innocent III never objected strenuously to his morals. He was not a genius in the use of governmental devices nor addicted to administrative innovations as was his father, though no one has yet explained the source of numerous administrative refinements occurring in his reign both in England and in Normandy, nor was he a military genius. Yet he was more nearly like his father and his brother than critics have been willing to admit. When the forces arrayed against him are fully weighed—the France of Philip Augustus, the Church of Innocent III, the barons who had known the machinations of Henry II and the avarice of Richard, the growing inadequacy of feudal finance and feudal military weapons for the needs of a monarchical state—the wonder is that he held out so long, not that he succumbed in the end. For the Europe of 1200 was not the Europe of 1066 just as Innocent III was not Hildebrand. Nor should one compare lightly the position of an English King in the full career of Philip Augustus with that of Henry II at his accession.

Of course John should have been a statesman. He should have comprehended the new forces which were rampant in the Europe of his day. He should have abandoned the extreme position of his forbears either against Philip or against the Church or against his barons. With one antagonist alone he might have been successful. Yet how could he foresee Boniface VIII, the Edwards, or the Tudors? How was he to know that his successors might enjoy advantages which he lacked?

Actually, his situation was hopeless from the start. He may not have used his resources to their utmost limit, though that has still to be demonstrated, but they were clearly insufficient. The one fact that stands out beyond dispute is his failure. Because he essayed the rôle of the Tudors long in advance of the special conditions which made the Tudor plans both successful and popular, the barons, the clergy, and the Pope all became his masters. Because he alone of European sovereigns pushed the fight against baron, clergy, and Pope simultaneously and to its ultimate conclusions, he reaped the full and bitter harvest of his own temerity. Yet it is also because of these reasons that the English monarchy became a limited monarchy as early as the thirteenth century; such it has remained, on the whole, be it remembered, from that day to this.

The details of John's relations with the Church and the clergy, in Ireland, in England, and in his continental lands, are overwhelming in their cumulative portrayal of violence and brutality. Limoges, Poitiers, Coutances, Séez, York, Winchester, and Lincoln all tell the same story of high-handed violence and the pillage of ecclesiastical revenues. Yet there was no open breach with Rome until 1206. Innocent III needed John in the imperial tangle. Philip Augustus was still recalcitrant in the affair of Ingeborg, and he was opposing the Pope strenuously in the German election. Even John's seizure of lands belonging to his widowed mother and sister-in-law brought only protests from the Pope, the defender of widows and orphans. When John repudiated his former wife and married Isabelle of Angoulême, whom he had stolen from her fiancé, the Count of Marche, the Pope did practically nothing, though the deed itself was the scandal of Europe. John confessed his sins to his archbishop, was assigned penance, and received absolution. This Innocent III confirmed by letter with many an admonition against the wiles of the flesh.

In the Norman dispute between Philip and Richard, later with John, Innocent III had been eager to mediate and had done so repeatedly but without success. The quarrel between Capetian and Plantagenet was not justiciable but rather a trial of strength with Normandy as the victor's prize. Neither side could or would listen to the Pope though each sought his help. But papal legates and papal letters could do little in the face of the relentless onrush of the troops of Philip Augustus. Even though Innocent III preferred not to see additional French conquests both he and John were virtually powerless. Château Gaillard fell in 1204 and with it the whole Norman defense.

The Norman clergy, under a particularly able Archbishop of Rouen, did nothing to prevent the French occupation of the Duchy, still smarting under John's violent measures at Séez and elsewhere. They did write to Innocent III for instructions as to their attitude toward the conquerors. Innocent's reply, dated in 1205, is a most remarkable document. Professing ignorance of exact conditions in Normandy, he advised its clergy to make their own decision regarding the future. Was he attempting in this way to save his own face or had he lost interest in events which he could not control? In any case, he dodged the real issue. The actual verdict which he sanctioned by his silence had nothing to do with considerations of right and justice in the abstract; it was clearly based upon force and the fortunes of war.

While John was still attempting unsuccessfully to rouse the barons and clergy of England for a gigantic effort against the French which would undo the events of 1204, Hubert Walter, Archbishop of Canterbury, died. John was very anxious to fill his place with a devoted follower, both because of the importance of the office and in view of the critical situation both at home and abroad. The resulting conflict with Innocent III lasted for eight years, made England a papal fief in 1213, and contributed powerfully to the forces which made England a limited monarchy two years later.

A faction of the monks of Christchurch elected one man while the remainder, under royal pressure, elected the King's candidate. Both parties sent delegates to Rome, as did also the suffragan bishops of the province who claimed a voice in the selection of their superior. Innocent III characteristically ruled that both elections were uncanonical and induced the delegates in Rome to elect a third person, Stephen Langton, a cardinal and an Englishman. Since John would not give his consent to this action, Innocent III consecrated Stephen Langton as Archbishop of Canterbury and Primate of all England, at Viterbo, in June, 1207. Within a month John's agents had evicted the Christchurch monks from England, substituted Augustinian friars in their places, and confiscated the domain and the revenues of the province of Canterbury.

The struggle thus inaugurated between Innocent III and John was no less the eternal warfare of medieval Pope and medieval Emperor than the earlier contest

between Gregory VII and Henry IV or the later conflict between Philip IV of France and Boniface VIII.
Only John's failure in the fight for the cause of the
secular State against the ecclesiastical Commonwealth
has obscured the issues at stake. Had he succeeded the
English people would doubtless cherish a seventh John
as much as a seventh Henry or a seventh Edward;
as it is John stands alone, of all the Kings since 1066,
and needs no distinguishing number.

John's weapons in the struggle were confiscation of
lands and revenue, taxation, and violence. Without
the sympathy of his people he could not mobilize the
latent antipathy to Rome which was undoubtedly present in England. Innocent III was armed with mightier
weapons which, in the trenchant phrase of Lea, "slew
the soul." The interdict was proclaimed for all England in 1208. Authorities still differ sharply as to
the precise form which it took but all are agreed that
of all the sacraments of the Church only baptism was
allowed. Even the sacraments of marriage and extreme unction were denied to all persons for the dura-
tion of the interdict. Burial could not take place in
consecrated ground. John countered with the seizure
of the goods and chattels of the clergy; near-by towns
were appointed as the custodians of this property and
authorized to allow the clergy only a minimum of
their resources for the purposes of food and shelter.
Innocent promptly excommunicated all persons who
should take any part in the enforcement of these arrangements. The higher clergy emigrated to the continent. Stephen Langton, not unmindful of Becket

and his fate and with little apparent enthusiasm for a martyr's crown, refused to cross the channel into England. In 1210 Innocent added to the pressure already being exerted by excommunicating John. The clergy still resident in England, refused, on the whole, to publish the bull of excommunication; John seems to have been quite indifferent to the whole matter.

It may seem strange that John could endure the interdict for five years when Philip Augustus did not succeed in holding out against it even for a full year. Several things must be borne in mind by way of explanation. The questions at stake in England were more vital than those which had arisen between Philip and the Pope. England was not as accessible as France to papal influence and papal emissaries. The interdict was probably never strictly observed at any one time throughout all England. Moreover, the whole struggle gave John enormous material gains at a time when the chief weakness of the English King was financial. With the confiscated revenues of the Church he could and did obtain mercenaries, raise troops, perfect a foreign coalition, and defy the barons and the towns who would otherwise have certainly placed some curb upon his excesses. The resources of the English state had never before been more completely in the hands of an English King than they were in the years of the interdict from 1208 to 1213. But they were not sufficient. When Innocent III took a further step in 1211 and released Englishmen from their allegiance to their sovereign, this action made as little difference to Englishmen as to John. His brutality and his violence, plus the obvious defects of his personal morals, had made him a lonely figure. His cause did not appeal to any great body of Englishmen even though a struggle against the Church should have produced a party for its leader.

There was but one thing left which Innocent III could do; he did it with evident reluctance. He deposed John from the English throne and offered his crown to Philip of France. The French army which was to enforce this decree would be a holy army, and the whole adventure was to take on the nature of a crusade. The substitution of Philip for John upon the English throne was to be a task on a par, in papal eyes, with the contest against the Saracen in Spain or against the heretic in southern France. This is the clearest possible example of the supremacy in secular affairs of the ecclesiastical ruler of Europe.

Yet Cardinal Pandolfo, papal legate in charge of the whole affair, continued his negotiations with John up to the last possible moment. In 1213 Philip Augustus had assembled his army at Boulogne; John had gathered his troops at Dover. Concurrently John had arranged an international coalition against Philip Augustus, later in evidence at Bouvines in the following year. Then, at the last moment, John yielded to the legate, preferring submission to the Pope to imminent defeat at the hands of Philip and a foreign army, supported by an expatriated clergy and by his own disgruntled nobles. Indeed the final straw seems to have been disaffection within the English army itself.

The surrender of John to the Pope was a complete

defeat, a literal abdication. Not only did he concede
every disputed point, such as the Canterbury election
and the question of ecclesiastical property, but he surrendered his crown to the papacy, put his state in the
domain of St. Peter, declared himself the Pope's man
for the territory of England and Ireland, and agreed
to an annual payment to the Pope of one thousand
marks. At last a great monarchy had openly acknowledged the papal theory of a European ecclesiastical
Commonwealth. As a result, from 1213 until John's
death and long afterwards, England was ruled by
papal legates.

John undoubtedly hoped to counterbalance all this,
as earlier in the case of Normandy, by subsequent
victories over his foes. He had high hopes of the
plans that led on to Bouvines. If he could have ruined
the Capetian house, restored the Empire in the hands
of Otto, and gained the personal prestige of a victory
against Philip of France and his allies, he might well
have arranged the affairs of Church and State in England to suit himself. John's defeat in Poitou in 1214
against the French and the debacle of his cherished
European coalition at Bouvines later in the same year
destroyed these phantasies forever.

Yet even this feudal dependence upon the Pope had
its uses. Innocent obtained mild terms from Philip
for his new vassal following Bouvines, while rejoicing
in the victory which displayed John's weakness and
at the same time gave papal plans the ascendancy in
the Empire and in Italy. Innocent III may have disliked the emphasis which these developments had

placed upon Philip Augustus but he was always dealing with a nice balance of contending forces. Complete victory for the papal position was unthinkable
in view of the situation in which Europe found itself.
From 1214 to 1216 Innocent III was at the height
of his own and of papal power in Europe and with
that he must needs have been content.

The next chapter in English history is brief but mo-
mentous. John returned to England to find that the
successive losses of prestige sustained by the crown
in 1204, in 1213, and now in 1214, were irreparable.
He was at the mercy of his baronial foes. Stephen
Langton himself, more English than Roman and
jealous of the legate, organized the resources of feudal
England against a man who had been so strong as to
trample upon their every right yet so weak as to sell
them body and soul to Rome. Again John tried to
capitalize his status as a papal vassal. He granted
free elections to the Church, with the papal confirmation. But the prelates were barons as well as churchmen. They insisted upon dealing decisively with their
overlord who had so frequently and so brutally gone
beyond the terms of his feudal contract or ignored
that contract altogether. Then John took the cross,
thus adding the inviolability of a crusader to his other
armor. But all to no avail. The barons proceeded
to military action, seized the royal courts, and ad-
vanced upon London. So John gave in once more
and at Runnymede, in 1215, sealed the Great Charter.

This is not the place for a careful appraisal of the
"palladium of English freedom" but its main character

may be briefly outlined. The Great Charter was a feudal charter of liberties not a national guarantee of liberty. It was a reactionary document which did little more than restate feudal customs and municipal rights as previously established but not observed. It "put the king below the law," but that law was feudal custom and its only sanction was armed rebellion. John wrote to the Pope that his submission to the papacy had made the Charter possible. Innocent responded as best he could, declaring the Charter null and void. The grounds upon which he took this action are not entirely clear but appear to have been the status of John as a crusader. As such the Church should protect his holdings, England, against all encroachments. It is significant for those who see innovation in the Great Charter that Innocent III, with all his legalist's hatred of novelty, did not attack the document on that ground as he abrogated it.

The barons who had proceeded to Runnymede because of the royal submission to the Pope, according to John's own statement, were even more incensed at Innocent's attempts to destroy the Great Charter and John's obvious determination to evade it. Taking a leaf from the book of papal strategy, they called in Louis, son of Philip Augustus, to occupy the English throne. The death of John in 1216 turned them back to the greater attractions of a minority; the death of Innocent III in the same year doubtless diminished their fear of government from Rome.

Innocent's success in his relations with England was all that one could wish but it must be pointed out that John's surrender was not as ignominious a defeat in 1213 as it seems to the modern world. Richard had acknowledged the feudal dependence of England upon the Empire; the Emperors themselves regularly took their crowns from the Pope. To become a papal vassal in an age which looked upon the feudal relationship as a perfectly normal one was hardly a mark of disgrace. If Englishmen felt that John had been false to England in taking his crown from the Pope, then they were thinking already, however haltingly, in those national terms which were alone to suffice as a check and a solvent for the papal policies which Innocent III personified. From John's point of view the submission to the Pope was merely one move in a game, a game which he played with all the reckless abandon of one who plays to win and for that alone.

EASTERN EUROPE

The interest of Innocent III in the affairs of the Magyar and Slav peoples in the east of Europe was very real. Their geographical position made them potential factors in the German contest for the imperial throne. They occupied the only overland route from Europe to Palestine. Partly affiliated with the Greek Orthodox Church and partly subordinate to Rome, they constituted a battleground for the rival organizations and the divergent cultures of the Eastern and the Western Churches. Finally, the political growth of their nascent states had at that time produced neither stability nor independence.

As usual, Innocent's plans were well-formulated. He meant to have Hungary and Serbia and Bulgaria as vassal states, dependent in religion and in politics upon Rome. By the Latinization of the Church in Serbia and in Bulgaria he meant to advance plans for a union of the two Churches, Greek and Roman. Furthermore, by dominating the lands between the Alps and the Carpathians, he meant to utilize their resources either for papal plans in Germany or for the much-desired crusade. In all of this he achieved more than a fair measure of success.

The Hungarian royal house boasted two saints, a sufficient commentary upon its amenability to the dictation of the successors of St. Peter. Innocent III, thanks to a disputed succession which gave him some of the same advantages in Hungary which he simultaneously enjoyed in the Empire, kept intact this tradition of loyalty to the Pope. The bulk of the Serbs inclined in religion as in politics to Constantinople. Minority parties, however, appealed respectively to Hungary and to the papacy. In the complicated negotiations which resulted Innocent III was not entirely successful although he devoted a good deal of attention to them throughout his pontificate; the Serb Church remained Greek and a Serbian crown bestowed with the papal blessing was not forthcoming until after the consecration of Innocent's successor.

In Bulgaria Innocent III found even more alluring possibilities. Only Hungarian interference prevented the Latinization of the Bulgarian Church subsequent to open acknowledgment of Bulgarian political dependence upon Rome. As it was, the Bulgarian King was crowned by a papal legate in 1204 and may be added, from that date, to the growing list of princes avowedly vassals of the Holy See.

The preëminence which Innocent III maintained in the east of Europe was due to very clever juggling of both religious and political factors. Here, perhaps more than elsewhere, he was a master of balance and bargain. For those devoted to him as churchman and moral leader, these pages from Innocent's career will not appear as attractive as some others, but they are equally typical. It may well be that his communications to the states in the east of Europe contain less of lofty language than those directed to the monarchs of western Europe; he faced totally different problems and circumstances in the two areas. In both the east of Europe and in the west, however, Innocent III was mainly and overwhelmingly absorbed in what seemed to him fundamentals, the perfection of the organization of the Roman Church and the enforcement of his conception of an ecclesiastical Commonwealth against all-comers, notably against the secular rulers of the day.

CHAPTER III

INNOCENT III AND THE CHURCH

INNOCENT III AND THE CRUSADES

Innocent III spent a large part of his official life preaching and planning for a great and successful crusade. It was the one thought always uppermost in his mind, the common denominator of all his projects and schemes. For it he sacrificed a variety of advantages in many parts of Europe. Yet the thing itself never occurred. It proved to be the one purpose of his life which was in no measure attained. The domestic crusades in Spain and in southern France were really beside the point, veritable punitive expeditions within the family circle. The Fourth Crusade was hardly an admirable affair on any reckoning, papal or otherwise; certainly it had little or nothing to do with the restoration of the Holy Places of Palestine to Christian control. The great crusade which Innocent summoned for 1216 missed fire completely. For this failure Innocent's own multifarious activities elsewhere in Europe are to be held partly responsible, but it is equally clear that the Europe of the thirteenth century had lost the crusading ardor so dominant a century earlier.

Both the Albigensian Crusade in southern France and the Fourth Crusade, however, were important events in the pontificate of Innocent III, reveal significant features of his relations with the secular rulers of Europe, and demonstrate both the enormous strength and the peculiar weaknesses of the ecclesiastical organization over which he presided.

The sunny valleys of the Rhone and the Garonne, long the center of a culture as promising as it was distinctive, were rather thoroughly impregnated with radical doctrines in religion by the end of the twelfth century. Some of these ideas were indigenous, some imported; some were fantastic, some sensible. Many of them had been sporadic enemies of the Church throughout its existence. All were subversive of ecclesiastical organization and authority. Frankly anti-sacerdotal, they challenged a worldly clergy with the tradition of apostolic poverty and the haughty occupant of St. Peter's throne with the humility of its Founder.

It is to be noted that this very territory, teeming with danger for the organized Church, was precisely that part of France, after 1204, which had most successfully resisted the centripetal force exerted by the Capetian Kings. The Count of Toulouse was here a great feudal lord in the manner of a William of Normandy or of a Henry the Lion. The political and ecclesiastical authorities of the early thirteenth century might waver a bit separately but they formed in combination a veritable Juggernaut as the Count of Toulouse proceeded to demonstrate, to the destruction of his house.

Of the many and varied beliefs in the south of

France in this period it has been customary to make a relatively simple classification. Some of their adherents were called Waldensians since they were followers of Peter Waldo, a rich merchant of Lyons who had caused certain parts of the Bible to be translated, given his goods to the poor, and led a movement toward a return to primitive Christianity. Indulgent Popes tolerated him and his followers; others persecuted them. In any case the sect spread rapidly into many parts of France. Posterity called their founder the St. Francis of heresy. They were recognized as Christian anti-sacerdotalists and discouraged and repressed as such, but no one ever tried to exterminate them, although individuals probably suffered in the days when heretic-baiting was a popular pastime in southern France. Remnants of the group, long since pushed back into the Alpine valleys of Provence, allied themselves with the sixteenth-century revolt against ecclesiastical machinery when it came. Indeed they were the precursors of the Reformation since they abandoned ecclesiastical practices not demonstrably apostolic and held the principle of the "priesthood of the Christian man," so dear to Wyclif and Luther alike.

The Albigensians, or *Cathari*, however, were of a different sort. Descended spiritually from Persian Manichæism, that duality of eternal good and eternal evil which St. Augustine was still so valiantly fighting in the fifth century, they substituted for the Christian religion totally different principles and completely contrasting rites. They believed in two gods, one good and one evil, the one in control of the spirit and the other in control of the flesh; the one appealing to the few who were capable of a perfect life, the other appealing to the many; both in perpetual conflict one with the other. In a half-poetic, half-rationalistic, but wholly Asiatic manner, they taught that a perfect life was self-centered and self-sufficient, completely celibate, absolutely untouched by the evils and blandishments of this world. Their best men, as a result, were so far superior to the clergy of southern France as to make the latter ridiculous. On the other hand, they discouraged the masses of men from any attempt to win heaven by good works or ritualistic expressions of faith. They recognized no purgatory and no hell for the spirit. They acknowledged Christ only as a man. Thus were the Catholic Church and the Catholic clergy discredited, their authority defied, and, more often than not, their abbeys and their churches plundered.

These ideas have been traced from their home in the Orient via the Greek, Slav, and Bulgarian peoples of the Balkan peninsula to Dalmatia and the coast towns of Italy and thence into southern France in the eleventh century through merchant and student channels. Henry II of England contemplated a joint crusade with the French King against them in 1178. Mission after mission entered Languedoc in the years following bent on the extirpation of this heresy and its adherents. All to little avail. By the end of the century the great feudal lords in the south were all either Albigensians themselves or tolerant of their teachings throughout their lands. Even Raymond VI, Count of Toulouse in 1194, though he remained a Catholic himself, allowed the Albigensian heresy to flourish from one end of his extensive territory to the other.

Innocent III was no fanatic but he saw rightly in the Albigensian teachings and example a serious impairment of the authority of the Church. Since his predecessors had neglected the problem because of difficulties with Henry VI and for other reasons, he proceeded to immediate action, but with caution and in due form. Law and equity were not empty names for him. Let inquests be held and reports be made. For punishment he had in mind the confiscation of property, banishment, and exclusion from burial in consecrated ground, not death. Here, as elsewhere, local enthusiasm and narrow-minded official zeal soon went beyond his control. Innocent III was the first of the Popes to rely extensively upon the secular arm in such matters and was therefore the first to discover how difficult it is to call back the hounds of violence once they are unleashed.

He tried persuasion first, both through legates and by direct appeals to the secular rulers. Results were disappointing. Repeated requests for aid from Philip Augustus were persistently refused on the ground of his difficulties with England. In 1207 Innocent III issued an appeal both to Philip Augustus and to the barons of France which was a frank call to a veritable crusade.

On the twelfth of January, 1208, a follower of the

Count of Toulouse symbolized the rampant opposition to the efforts of the Church to stamp out heresy in Languedoc by the murder of Peter of Castelnau, the legate of the Pope. No reagent could have precipitated more quickly or more sharply the various forces and passions previously in solution than this mad act of violence. Raymond VI was almost certainly entirely innocent of any complicity in a murder which was at the same time such an unthinkable crime and such a direct attack upon the Church and its leader, yet it sealed his fate and that of his house. Innocent III at once released the subjects of the Count of Toulouse from their allegiance and invited the warriors of Christendom to occupy and guard his lands.

Philip Augustus protested this action and asserted that he alone, as overlord, had the right to occupy the fief of Toulouse under such circumstances. He also pointed out that there had been no formal condemnation of Raymond as a heretic. Raymond VI, conscious of his dangerous position (not unlike that in which Henry II of England had found himself on the morrow of Becket's murder), went through all the forms of submission, professed his orthodoxy, and promised to suppress heresy throughout his lands, all to the accompaniment of the full ceremonial of the Church in the manner of Canossa.

The party of action, however, had already placed an army in the field to stamp out heresy in the south. The command was in the hands of a legate but most of the great churchmen and barons of France were in the host. Béziers was taken and put to the fire and sword as an example of the fate which God had in store for heretics and the protectors of heretics. "Kill them all, God will know His own" has reëchoed down the centuries as the slogan of the conflict which ensued, an accurate though doubtless an apocryphal description of the action of the ecclesiastical army. Massacre followed massacre with all the cruelty which perverted fanaticism could devise. Reports of miracles on both sides seemed to put the seal of divine approbation upon the blood-thirsty fury of the mob.

Many of the crusaders, of course, vented their rage upon the comparatively defenseless inhabitants of the south and departed for their homes at the end of forty days, carrying with them only the booty incidental to any successful armed expedition. Others looked forward to the permanent conquest of lands so miraculously opened to orthodox warriors. Simon de Montfort, whose family held lands in France, in Normandy, and in England, became Viscount of Béziers and Carcassonne and the lay ruler of the crusade. Raymond VI of Toulouse, fresh from his submission to the papal legate, hardly dared lead the baronial opposition to the papal army in the south, but the rapidity and the extent of De Montfort's conquests goaded him into action in the end. As a result, by 1212, he found himself practically stripped of all his possessions.

At this point even Innocent III felt that matters had gone too far. Raymond VI had never been convicted of heresy; the crusading army acted under the authority of the Pope and was presumably com-

missioned only against heresy and heretics. Moreover, Innocent III disliked the excesses of the army
and the growing power of De Montfort. His legates
on the spot, however, forced the papal hand or dis-
obeyed papal instructions, as the occasion seemed to
warrant. They had committed themselves irretrieva-
bly to the most extreme ecclesiastical position and had
allowed themselves to become inextricably entangled
in feudal schemes and political trickery. Even to stop
the crusade was for them retreat, alike unthinkable and
impossible. They were ardent devotees of war to
the finish; they contemplated complacently the literal
extermination of the heretics of southern France. De
Montfort and his associates were equally anxious to
continue a war which was the occasion and the justi-
fication of their extensive and expanding territorial
acquisitions. The Pope found it the more difficult to
act since he had accepted gifts from the conquerors
and confirmed the majority of their conquests.

Actual hostilities ceased in 1213 but no decision
concerning the lands of Raymond VI was forthcoming until the Lateran Council of 1215. The churchmen who had painted Raymond as the devil incarnate
insisted that he be deprived of all his property, but
Innocent III, tender of right and justice and devoted
as always to a policy of balance, decreed that Raymond should retain his lands beyond the Rhone which
the crusaders had not conquered and held out hopes
to his son that he might one day regain the remainder
of his patrimony. Eventually the lands of Toulouse
were given to the French crown by an inheritance

treaty practically dictated by the Church to the parties concerned in 1229. The Capetians, who had done little or nothing in connection with the crusade in the south, gathered all its fruits.

It would be idle to deny the Albigensian Crusade as a measure of Innocent III. He opposed its worst features, to be sure, but it was a papal project. It stamped upon the eternal principles of justice and it trampled upon common decency and humanity. It suggested the impossibility of a crusade unless perverted with ulterior and mundane objectives. It also displayed the Pope incompletely master in his own house. More than all else, it gave an enormous impetus to heresy-hunting, foretold the rigors of the Inquisition (largely a papal product), and prefigured the stakes with their blazing faggots in the lurid light of which Europe was to view its own bigotry and intolerance for fully five centuries.

The Fourth Crusade was a movement even less pleasing to Innocent III on every count. To a very considerable extent a Venetian enterprise, though composed largely of French nobles, its first exploit was the capture for Venice of the Christian town of Zara, the property of that King of Hungary whom Innocent considered his son and vassal. Its main achievement turned out to be the conquest of the remnants of the Byzantine Empire. The agreement of the Venetians and the French barons to share equally the patriarchal and imperial offices in the Latin Empire thus established shows in a flash the real purposes and character of the Fourth Crusade and its protagonists.

Surely no Pope, Innocent III least of all, could sanction any movement so clearly secular in its purposes and so little calculated to ensure general peace or serve papal policies, even though it did deck itself with the trappings of a crusade and camouflage itself as a holy work.

Yet Innocent III avoided a complete break with the crusaders. He saw in their project possibilities of another kind. The conquest of the Byzantine Empire by a western army meant the subjection of the eastern clergy during the occupation and perhaps the eventual union of the two Churches, then formally separated for a century and a half. Innocent III was not the only Pope to be allured by the hope of uniting the Eastern and Western Churches, but he is the only one who actually used frankly military and political agencies for the purpose.

He condemned the Zara episode, but not too caustically. Later, just as the crusaders left for Constantinople, he absolved them from the consequences of their sin. He did not support the march on Constantinople but he did not condemn it. He accepted the Latin Empire set up in 1204 and the submission to himself of its clergy, but he would not confirm the agreement of the Venetians and the French nobles to divide the spoil. He reproved the French for the violence incidental to the capture of the city, but he accepted valuable presents selected from the booty and even visited the interdict upon Genoa because its fleet had stolen those objects while they were being transported to Rome.

The two projects which were to justify such curious compromises with right and justice were not successful. Innocent III did not Latinize the Greek Church in the old Byzantine Empire and his best efforts did not suffice to unite the Eastern and the Western Churches. In each case the cause was probably a hopeless one. Nine centuries have now demonstrated that the Greek and the Latin Churches differed on essential points and that their members were truly men of divergent spirits. An additional handicap for Innocent III, however, was the tactlessness of his legates and agents; their attempts to produce immediate results antagonized the Greek clergy and solidified their resistance to the Roman Church. The four canons of the Fouth Lateran Council which are devoted to the question of the union of the two Churches hardly do more than bear witness to the futility of the whole project.

Innocent III undoubtedly hoped to counterbalance all ills with another and a more successful crusade. The earlier plans by which he had already achieved a position as overlord in the Kingdom of Jerusalem, in Antioch, in Armenia, and in Cyprus were by no means abandoned. He made every effort, after 1205, to secure a general pacification in the east which should make a crusading movement possible. Nor did he neglect the European side. The ten years preceding 1215 saw legates and others preaching a crusade at every cross-roads in the west. But Innocent III was obviously thinking in terms of the First Crusade, not the Fourth. He wanted a levy *en masse*. This proved very confusing to those entrusted with secular government and even to those in charge of ecclesiastical administration. Philip Augustus attempted to limit by legislation the amount of interference in the ordinary routine of government which might be allowed a Pope who was preparing for a crusade.

Innocent III called loudly for a crusade at the Lateran Council in 1215 and a number of its canons were devoted to the details involved. But there was no crusade. The nobles of Europe would not go under any conditions which the Church could sanction; the mob may have been willing, but it was leaderless. Innocent III, however, kept calling for a crusade to the day of his death, not perceiving with posterity that the thirteenth century was little likely to produce crusades or crusaders, except such men as the Emperor Frederick II whom the Church would denounce as a prince of sinners or King Louis IX of France whom all the world would acclaim as a saint.

INNOCENT III AND HIS ECCLESIASTICAL SUBORDINATES

Innocent III did not deal exclusively with powerful kings, scheming princes, defiant crusaders, heretics, or Italian towns; a very large part of his energy was devoted to churchmen and to purely ecclesiastical problems. Living as he did in the age of the Great Charter he could not afford to ignore the potential strength which lurked in the hands of the bishops of the Church. They were scattered, to be sure, but capable of union. It was possible that their authority rested upon as divine a sanction and upon as aged a tradition as that of Rome itself. The growth of France and England in the thirteenth century as political entities offered an excuse and an opportunity for episcopal solidarity by national groups. Innocent III stood squarely upon the Isidorian principle that episcopal power was a power delegated by the papacy; he was himself largely responsible for the eventual triumph of this theory.

He never claimed the right to appoint all the higher clergy of the Church but he came very near doing so in practice. Theoretically he never interfered with the freedom of election under normal conditions but normal conditions were scarcely the rule in the medieval Church. Thus he took it upon himself to decide as to the suitability of all candidates for the offices concerned, to interfere if a vacancy lasted too long, and to make the appointment himself if the previous incumbent had died at Rome. Moreover, he declared the union between a bishop and his diocese was so close that only the Pope could break it; hence depositions, resignations, and translations from one see to another were entirely in his hands. As a result he controlled the worst offenders in the episcopacy by deposing them from their offices and at the same time checked the budding careers of many ecclesiastical "go-getters" who would have preferred to exchange one diocese for another more wealthy or more famous. Nor was other evidence of episcopal dependence upon Rome lacking. The Pope confirmed or annulled episcopal decrees as he pleased. An archbishop had no authority as such until he had received the symbol of his rank, the *pallium,* from the Pope or from his legate. The papal court was an appellate court for every episcopal court in Christendom. In the endless disputes between bishops and cathedral chapters Innocent III usually supported the latter.

The appointment of members of the Roman clergy to prebends and benefices regardless of their geographical location was a device by which Innocent III attempted both to support his adherents from the bounty of the Church and at the same time to distribute his followers in every corner of western Europe. Bishops and chapters alike protested vehemently. The local authorities resented bitterly both the intrusion of papal nominees and the draining off of local resources for the papal entourage.

Innocent III was also interested in the parish priest and in his problems. He attempted to enforce for the entire priesthood the canonical prerequisites of a legitimate birth, a sound body, and a blameless life. He made heroic efforts to abolish simony and to enforce celibacy for the parish priests as well as for their ecclesiastical superiors. He used every influence to compel the payment of tithes. The undue prolongation of a vacancy in a parish and the knotty question of the subdivision of parishes and the creation of new livings were as likely to engage his attention as a dispute which involved prelates.

One of the greatest difficulties which confronted Innocent III in the government of the Church was a purely physical one. He could not hope to be present simultaneously in the great centers of the Church outside Rome or even consecutively in the course of one short pontificate, or perhaps at all in view of the shifting political fortunes of Italy and adjacent lands which made all travel uncertain if not actually unsafe. He did not leave Italy after his consecration. His influence, then, was exerted throughout Europe either by documents emanating from the papal Chancery or by agents.

The most efficient Chancery in Europe was at his disposal and the thousands of letters extant from his pontificate afford abundant evidence of its abilities. These letters are as incisive and as lucid as Innocent III himself. No other person in Europe could have dispatched so many letters or such able ones. No other person in Europe could have been so confident that his letters would be delivered, understood, and obeyed. Many of them, of course, dealt with the great problems of the day but scores of them were concerned with minor points of faith or morals, even with petty details of the ritual or of Biblical criticism. The demands which the modern world would put upon the question-box columns of both secular and religious periodicals or upon the question-box hour by radio were visited upon Innocent III. He was expected to pontificate with learning and with authority upon literally every question under the sun. To these appeals, apparently, he never turned a deaf ear, but patiently culled the relevant passages from the Scriptures and from the Fathers to produce an answer which seldom failed to satisfy both himself and his correspondent. Time and again he restrained the local clergy from action which would have been unwise though superficially in accord with the teachings of the Church. Here he was ever the jurist and the philosopher, drawing upon an apparently inexhaustible store of experience and evincing a notable skill in administrative procedure.

Letters are but scraps of paper even when they are also papal bulls and in them the full tone of Innocent's authority upon many questions could never have found adequate expression. Thus he relied more and more upon legates as the agents of his will. Chosen from the clergymen whom he knew intimately and carefully schooled in the papal traditions, these men performed the most difficult tasks for the Pope, far from Rome. They acted as the Pope himself and were clothed with his full authority within the limits of their commissions. Legates dealt with John and with Philip of France, negotiated with Bulgarian princes and infidel rulers, directed the Albigensian Crusade and attempted to direct the Fourth Crusade, delivered papal *ultimata* in Spain, in Galicia and in Armenia, and acted as regents in Sicily, in Aragon, and in England.

Innocent III was not the first to use legates extensively nor the last but he displayed more fully than did any other Pope the possibilities of such officials as papal agents. Yet even Innocent III could not entirely control his own tools. The legates superseded all local officials of whatever rank; their instructions were frequently exceedingly vague. Often they could not report to their papal master at anything like suitable intervals. Almost without exception they were men of energy and initiative, over-zealous for the accomplishment of the purposes for which they had been sent. It is not surprising that they went beyond the papal program upon many occasions and committed the Pope to measures which he could neither approve nor abandon. These officials point to the unity of the universal Church and they did constitute a remarkably effective channel through which papal authority was transmitted to its remote corners, but they were not an unmitigated blessing for the Holy See.

The papal Curia itself presented difficulties. Innocent III insisted that his court was an appellate court for every civil and criminal tribunal in Christendom whenever ecclesiastical persons or subjects were involved. In an age when marriage was a sacrament and a broken contract of any kind a sin, this was tantamount to complete appellate jurisdiction. These claims were doubtless based upon the Pseudo-Isidorian Decretals and upon a false reading of the Theodosian Code but the energy of Innocent III virtually read them into the law of Europe. Pope Martin V gave up the claim to appellate jurisdiction for secular courts in 1418; the authority of the papal Curia over all ecclesiastical courts has never been relinquished.

The business which normally came before the papal Curia was voluminous. Litigation was slow; the court was venal. Innocent III recognized the worst of these evils and tried to correct them. He evicted the money-changers from the halls of the Lateran palace and forbade all gifts to the Curia in advance of its decisions. The accounts of Matthew Paris and other contemporaries, however, would indicate that papal reforms in this direction as in others were few and unimportant. Government was costly then as now. Justice, in the medieval view of life, was closely linked with finance. Innocent III experimented a little with other devices for procuring revenue for the Church, but the problem was really left to his successors. His own generosity to churchmen and to others may very well have contributed to the high cost of papal justice though he himself, especially by comparison with the multifarious concerns of the enormous institution of which he was the head, lived very quietly and simply either at the Lateran or, in summer, in one of the hill towns of the Roman Campagna.

He did take an intense, personal interest, nevertheless, in the affairs of the Curia, participated regularly in its deliberations, and produced a reasonable dispatch of the more important cases which came before it.

The outstanding characteristics of Innocent III as head of the Church were his broad outlook and his very great administrative skill. His was the legal mind, yet he had a remarkable comprehension of the adjustments and compromises which actual government usually requires. He was no fanatic. In his hands papal theories crystallized more precisely but papal procedure gained in vigor and in flexibility. He was an incomparable administrator when administration was commonly a matter of chance. Henry II of England and Philip Augustus of France had perhaps already tapped the same sources which furnished Innocent III aid and comfort, notably the revived study of Justinian's Civil Law, but one has only to compare the scope and validity of the influences radiating from London, from Paris, and from Rome in the year 1216 to see the unique position which Innocent III actually occupied in the history of European government and, above all, in the history of the Roman Catholic Church as a governmental institution.

THE FOURTH LATERAN COUNCIL

The cap and climax of the pontificate of Innocent III was the Fourth Lateran Council of 1215, reckoned twelfth among the general Councils of the Western Church. Not only does it coincide almost exactly with the end of Innocent's rule chronologically but it sums up the accomplishments of his career, rounding off sharply each of the great problems which had engaged his attention as Pope and consecrating as law and precedent both the principles upon which his pontificate rested and the administrative arrangements to which these principles gave rise.

It is clear that this Council marks the end of a whole phase of growth in Europe and in the Church. The thirteenth century, as every one knows, found new problems which eventually exerted their influences upon Church and State alike. The resources of the Church, in theory and in procedure, with which, for good or ill, it attempted to solve these newer and vital questions are described and defined by the Fourth Lateran Council. Without this Council or without Innocent

III whose personality it reflects, the Church might have met these problems in some other way. The Fourth Lateran Council displayed to the Church its own resources but it also tied the Church down to the policies and activities of the past. Its importance can hardly be overestimated. St. Thomas Aquinas will one day cite the authority of this Council against that of Gratian. The great Mendicant Orders, the Franciscans and the Dominicans, will bear witness to its prestige by the assiduity with which they will fabricate and maintain the legend of their foundation by it.

The call for this Council went forth from the Lateran in April, 1213, while Innocent III was still flushed with his resounding successes against John and against Otto. He placed the date of meeting far enough ahead to make possible the extraordinarily large attendance for which he hoped. While his cherished ambition of a Council composed of at least two bishops from each ecclesiastical province in Christendom, plus all the primates and patriarchs, together with representatives from all secular states and the most important municipal corporations, was not realized, still the membership of the Council was both numerous and distinguished. About thirteen hundred prelates were present, including seventy-one primates and archbishops, in addition to numerous delegates from other ecclesiastical persons and groups, and representatives from the Sicilian Kingdom, the Latin Empire, France, England, Hungary, Jerusalem, Cyprus, Aragon, and from many other states. Surely this Council spoke of right with an authority not equaled since the great Council at Nicæa in the fourth century.

The work of the Council was ostensibly dispatched in three plenary sessions, in honor of the Trinity, on the eleventh, twentieth, and thirtieth of November respectively. It is clear, however, that so large a body could not debate effectively if at all. These formal sessions were devoted to a sermon by Innocent III, to an account by the Patriarch of Jerusalem of the terrible conditions in the near east, to a dramatic promulgation of the judgment against Raymond of Toulouse, to a condemnation of the heresy of Joachim of Flora, to the confirmation of the election of the Emperor Frederick II, and to the reading of the seventy-one canons of the Council. The actual work of the Council, as is the modern practice, was accomplished in committee and in conference prior to the final session. Granted that there was plenty of opportunity for the prelates to discuss certain questions in the conference room in advance of the publication of decisions, it is still difficult to escape the conclusion that this was Innocent's Council. He called it and he presided over it. He prepared its agenda, directed its procedure, and confirmed its canons. The Council exudes his authority at every point.

One or two cautions seem necessary before any attempt is made to evaluate accurately the work of this Council. Innocent III understood perfectly that this was an important moment in the history of the Church. Councils were rare at best and this one possessed a truly notable membership. He therefore included some things merely to give them a footing, others that traditions might be maintained. On the other hand, many matters found their way into the deliberations of the Council not because the Pope was especially interested in them or considered them particularly vital, but because they were immediate problems somewhere in the Church and clamored for an immediate decision.

Furthermore, the canons most interesting to the modern student were unquestionably not the most important in the eyes of the prelates of 1215. The latter were intensely interested in the preparatory arrangements for a crusade, in the action taken against Raymond of Toulouse, in the stipulation that the Jews in western Europe should henceforth wear a distinctive dress, in the condemnation of Joachim of Flora and his radical teachings, in the diminution of the prohibited degrees for canonical marriage from five to four, in the prohibition of all new monastic orders, and in the efforts of the Church to procure for itself an intelligent and celibate clergy. These things would cause a considerable stir in the synods of western Europe when they were formally promulgated by responsible ecclesiastical officials; all related to current and burning questions, many of them still actively in dispute. Yet we may dismiss them all with hardly a notice. The arrangements for a crusade, however interesting to the student of finance and administrative procedure, are really worthless since the crusade never came off. Even the failure of a great Council to hurl Europe into

Asia by legislation, or even to preserve universal peace by the same method for four short years as a predisposing condition, was as little instructive to the thirteenth as it has been to succeeding centuries. One may note that Innocent III was still less severe than the majority of his subordinates against Raymond of Toulouse; on this point alone the Council seems really to have guided his action, doubtless estimating more accurately than he the high passions and the bloody actions involved, though it is perhaps noteworthy that the decision did not constitute a canon of the Council but was merely a papal decision promulgated before the assembly. As for the other things, they are all matters of routine or clearly dependent upon previous decisions.

The real importance of the Council lies rather in the crown and seal placed by it upon papal supremacy in the Church and upon ecclesiastical supremacy in the lives of all men, together with the subtle but clear implication of papal infallibility. The unprejudiced reader who runs through its canons at a single sitting will be much impressed by the successive provisions which collectively describe a monarchical Church with many of the functions of a state; those already familiar with the pontificate of Innocent III will be prepared for the recurrent expressions which these canons contain both of his domination of the institution which he ruled and of its supremacy in human affairs in all Christendom. The statement that the rule of Innocent III marks the zenith of the Church as an ecclesiastical organization and the high point of the asserted superiority of the priesthood over the laity is not merely a theory nor a mistaken phantasy; it is patent in the official record of this Council. A summary of the contents of these canons from this point of view may do their author an injustice, since it disturbs the order in which he caused them to be listed, but it will reveal with cumulative force the interpretation which has just been placed upon them.

The Pope is supreme in the Church and has as his subordinates the Patriarchs of Constantinople, Alexandria, Antioch, and Jerusalem, in order. The Greek Church is subordinate to the Roman. Jews are to exist only under special conditions, including a distinctive costume, non-appearance upon the streets of a town on festal days, and ineligibility for all public offices. Heresy is defined and the responsibility for hunting out the heretics in each diocese is placed directly upon its bishop. The secular arm is to coöperate in the punishment of convicted heretics, under pain of ecclesiastical censures; the death penalty, by fire or otherwise, is not mentioned.

Vacancies in ecclesiastical offices are to be filled promptly and with suitable persons, without lay interference of any kind. The clergy may not be taxed by the state. Legislation harmful to the Church and its interests is *ipso facto* null and void. Laymen are to pay tithes as assessed, interfere not at all in the courts of the Church, present suitable persons as parish priests when they possess the patronage, and leave the incumbents, once appointed, severely alone.

Annual synods are to be held in each diocese to protect the Church from pluralism, simony, commercialism in its various forms, military or surgical activity on the part of churchmen, and from excesses in clerical drink, dress, or conduct. Instruction is to be provided for the clergy in each diocese since the cure of souls is the art of arts. Each archiepiscopal city is to have a Master of Theology in residence. Episcopal indulgences are valid only for a year. Relics may be authenticated only from Rome. New orders of monks are prohibited and those already in existence are to hold annual assemblies for the correction of monastic abuses.

Transubstantiation, that interpretation of the Eucharist which holds that its elements, bread and wine, are miraculously transformed into the body and blood of Christ, is formally stated for the first time. A physician must summon a priest to minister to the soul of his patient before he attempts to deal with his body. Every member of the Church, from the age of discretion, must confess his sins orally to his parish priest at least once a year, participating subsequently in the sacrament of the Mass, preferably at Easter.

Several of these canons are obviously of the greatest importance. Those dealing with the treatment of heretics virtually established the medieval Inquisition, although notable modifications were to come from succeeding pontificates before the days of its greatest success and worst excesses. The formulation of transubstantiation was an important step in setting the clergy apart as a necessary and distinctive group as well as an effective method of binding the laity to the Church in an inescapable manner. The canon that all secular laws which infringe upon the Church are null and void, though a literal interpretation would restrict its application only to laws promulgated by excommunicated secular officials, really epitomizes the Middle Ages. Disputed and contested it certainly was, perhaps otherwise it would not have been included in the canons of this Council, but there it was, a permanent challenge to every secular state in Europe and a perpetual source of inspiration for the Church.

The canon which required an annual auricular confession from every adult Christian and subsequent participation in the Eucharist was without doubt the master-stroke of the Council. This was an innovation in theory as well as in procedure, although the schoolmen had long indicated it as the logical and inevitable corollary of the sacrament of penance. The Church was probably not ready for this new departure either in its organization or in its personnel, but by it the soul of every living person in Europe was delivered into the hands of the parish priest. The power of the keys was no longer to be a theory debated at Rome or among the learned; it actually existed in the hands of the humblest member of the priesthood. The Church was the sole means to salvation, both necessary and efficacious for each repentant human being. But the latter must walk the path which the Church indicated. He must avoid heresy, confess his sins orally to his parish priest at least once a year, and partake of the Communion; for the latter and for the other sacraments of the Church the presence of a priest was essential except under the most unusual circumstances.

This formed doubtless the minimum requirement laid by the Church upon the individual, certainly there was a good deal more both to the Church and to the Christian life which it expected its members to lead, but this much was sufficient to display the power of the Church and to indicate its necessary and intimate connection with every human being.

It is true that a century of explanation and coercion followed the promulgation of this canon. It was necessary to educate priests as confessors, provide penitential codes, and enforce the seal of silence upon the confessional.   An endless argument over details was scarcely concluded at Trent in the sixteenth century, yet the canon was enforced, on the whole, despite the new burdens which it placed upon clergy and laity alike. For the coercive measures of the Church were potent ones. He who did not confess his sins could not participate in the sacraments of the Church nor could his body find burial in consecrated ground. Such a person found the only avenue for his soul's salvation permanently and effectively blocked.

The cumulative effect of the canons of the Fourth Lateran Council is stupendous. The monarchical organization of the Church is perfected, its superiority over the State asserted, and its control over every human being assured.   One must have been either heretic or believer in the Europe of 1215; in either case the ecclesiastical organization was intimately and adequately concerned. This is not the place to debate the good or bad qualities of such an institution, but rather to display its complexity, its guidance by certain far-reaching principles, and its truly extraordinary efficiency.

Historians of dissent will equal the contemporaries of Innocent III in their interest in the theories of Joachim of Flora and others who were in conflict with the established ecclesiastical system of their day, but the historian of Europe in its general aspects will linger rightly over the organization which was designed for the majority and accepted by it. The Church lost its control over the secular states of Europe, on the whole, by the end of the thirteenth century and it was obliged to observe the successful establishment of alternative paths to salvation in the sixteenth, although it refused to admit their validity. The central facts which are patent in the canons of this Council, on the other hand, have never been abandoned. The ecclesiastical principles codified in 1215 still obtain in the Roman Church. The career of Innocent III and the achievements of his pontificate embodied in the decisions of this Council were important factors in making possible this superb consistency. A Protestant historian may well pause to point out that only principles uncommonly well suited to the majority of men could have had the stamina to survive the repeated assaults of time and reason which have been heaped upon them. It was a happy chance that the ideas of the medieval Church, caught up in their full vigor, should have been reduced to writing at the dawn of the thirteenth century.

It is true that the modern world owes the intellectual organization of Catholic doctrine to St. Thomas Aquinas, but the foundation upon which he stood, an organized monarchical Church, was the work of Innocent III. The latter, more than any other single person, guaranteed its preservation, in all essentials, through the centuries. Yet Innocent III was a contemporary of that John who submitted to the Great Charter and of that Frederick II who demonstrated by the failure of an able man that World-Empire was impossible.

At the conclusion of the final session of the Fourth Lateran Council the attending prelates paid their respects individually to its presiding officer and requested leave to depart to their respective homes. Perhaps they should have been surprised to find that such permission turned upon a considerable present or offering. Actually they took it very much as a matter of course. The papacy was a thirteenth-century institution under Innocent III and it utilized the methods of its time. Gratuities to high officials on great occasions were always in order. It remained for the Popes of the Avignonese "Captivity" in the fourteenth century to make this custom systematic and burdensome.

From the close of the Council until July, 1216, Innocent III was as active as ever in the duties of his office. His relations with Philip Augustus became even more strained in this period due to their absorbing but conflicting interests in England. Whether the impending struggle would have crowned Innocent's career with a great victory over France or, as is more likely,

have revealed the hollowness of the strictly political
ascendancy which he seemed to possess, was not to be
demonstrated. Death intervened suddenly at Perugia
upon the sixteenth of July, 1216, in the fifty-fifth year
of the pontiff. He was buried in the basilica at Perugia
but his body now rests in the basilica of St. John
Lateran, the seat of his power, placed there by that
Pope who, in modern times, has most admired his
career, Leo XIII.

CONCLUSION

The significance of Innocent III in the history of western Europe is clear. No person since Charlemagne has been equally dominant in so many and in such important phases of its life and thought. No successor upon the papal throne has ever successfully revived the ecclesiastical Commonwealth of Europe which Innocent III postulated and, to a very considerable extent, enforced. He elaborated the principles of sacerdotal government and placed them upon an intelligent basis. As a legislator in the Church, as an ecclesiastical administrator, or as a temporal ruler, his fame is equally secure. His personal piety was never challenged; his sincerity may be demonstrated effectively. More judicious than Gregory VII, milder in temperament than Alexander III, with a detachment almost Jovian, he was for the papacy what Frederick Barbarossa had been for the Empire, an ideal and an example. Nor did he outlive his glory. He died in the prime of life, his physical and mental vigor unimpaired and his authority, on the whole, undiminished.

He was not, however, a popular figure among his contemporaries. Some were terrified by his marvelous memory, his truly remarkable knowledge of the Scriptures and the canons, or by the dogged persistence with which he pursued his objectives. Others were alienated by the intrigues and compromises of which he was a master. Even a Pope could hardly expect to negotiate with the infidel with complete impunity. But the majority of his enemies had fallen athwart the theocratic government which he had so successfully projected into the most remote corners of Europe. The biting verses of Walther von der Vogelweide are anti-sacerdotal and anti-Italian. The more sober strictures of English and imperial chroniclers were obviously occasioned by practical experience with ecclesiastical tyranny both in the Church and in the State. The Church itself, while profiting enormously by Innocent's achievements and following persistently though feebly in his footsteps, has never seen fit to canonize him. He was indubitably the ablest of the medieval Popes, but the saints of the thirteenth century are Francis and Aquinas, not Innocent III.

A great deal of the tangible success of Innocent III has, of course, proved transitory. We now know that the national State was to triumph over the non-national Church. We now know that Frederick II was as Ghibelline as any of his ancestors. We now know that Innocent's policies in Italy and in the Empire meant anarchy and disunion for those unhappy countries far down into the modern period, that his plans for France and for England were foredoomed to failure, and that his schemes for a union of the two Churches and for a greater crusade were completely futile.

On the other hand, the achievements of Innocent III as an administrator and as a legislator have stood the test of time. He consciously reverted to the age of the great Councils and summoned an ecumenical

Council which restated the faith and defined the practices of the Church. In it he prepared the machinery of the medieval Inquisition and defined transubstantiation. If Gibbon has seen in these two things the greatest triumph over sense and humanity that mankind has ever witnessed, others have seen in them the most far-reaching decrees of the medieval Church. Transubstantiation was the only dogma added by ecumenical authority to the Church in the Middle Ages and it still remains the central mystery of the ritual of the Roman Church. On it and the annual confessional the Church has lived from that day to this. The latter has always been the most effective device by which the Church has asserted and maintained its control over laymen.

The accomplishments and the authority of the Fourth Lateran Council, however, rested squarely upon the political career of Innocent III. His power came from the organization over which he presided, an organization which he expanded and strengthened by means of political activities. This organization, be it remembered, he left behind him.

No Pope since Innocent III has failed to rule a monarchical Church. No Pope since Innocent III has been able to think exclusively in religious terms; it must be admitted that few seem to have tried to do so. He fastened upon the papal office, for good or ill, the enticing and diverting idea of world-leadership. Neither the great Emperors of the Middle Ages nor the great heretics of the sixteenth century, neither Napoleon nor Garibaldi, have succeeded in uprooting the idea, now the conviction of millions of men, that the Pope is somehow a world-figure.

Centuries from now the schoolboy will be spared much if he still struggles with the history of western Europe during the first two thousand years of the Christian era, but not the name of Innocent III. His pontificate marks an important stage in the development of the Roman Catholic Church, a remarkable, an important, and a venerable human institution. Moreover, he contributed powerfully to that secular civilization in western Europe which is part and parcel of our common heritage, a civilization which he in part despised, in part combated, but in major part controlled.

BIBLIOGRAPHICAL NOTE

THE voluminous letters of Innocent III, together with his sermons and the *De contemptu mundi,* have been conveniently but rather inadequately edited by J. P. Migne in four volumes, *Innocentii III Romani Pontificis opera omnia* (Paris, 1889-1891), in his *Patrologiæ cursus completus, series latina,* Vols. CCXIV-CCXVII. The essential secondary account of Innocent III, virtually supplanting all others, is that of Achille Luchaire, *Innocent III* (6 vols., Paris, 1904-1908). The first five volumes deal successively with *Rome et l'Italie, La croisade des Albigeois, La papauté et l'empire, La question de l'Orient,* and *Les royautés vassales du Saint-Siège;* the sixth volume is devoted to *Le concile de Latran et la réforme de l'église* and contains an excellent bibliography and a general index of the whole work. The work of Friedrich von Hurter, *Geschichte Papst Innocenz III und seiner Zeitgenossen* (4 vols., Hamburg, 1834-1842), is too detailed for the general reader and somewhat out of date; the rather fantastic account of C. H. C. Pirie-Gordon, *Innocent the Great* (London, 1907), throws together a mass of useful information but is otherwise of little value.

Good brief accounts of Innocent III and his pontificate may be found in *The Catholic Encyclopedia* (good bibliography and map), in H. H. Milman, *History of Latin Christianity* (9 vols., London, 1883), in P. Schaff, *History of the Christian Church* (7 vols., New York, 1882-1910), in A. Flick, *The Rise of the Mediæval Church* (New York, 1909), and in E. Emerton, *Mediæval Europe* (New York, 1894). The most recent general textbooks dealing with Europe in the medieval period are G. C. Sellery and A. C. Krey, *Medieval Foundations of Western Civilization* (New

York, 1929), and E. M. Hulme, *The Middle Ages* (New York, 1929); they both contain chapters upon the period of Innocent III and excellent suggestions for further reading.

The Cambridge Medieval History has not yet reached the pontificate of Innocent III, but interesting material concerning the earlier part of Innocent's career may be found in the chapter upon Henry VI (Vol. V, ch. xiv). Volume VI entitled "Victory of the Papacy" and dealing with the thirteenth century is announced for publication in the fall of 1929. Additional material of considerable interest for the whole pontificate will be found in F. Gregorovius, *History of the City of Rome in the Middle Ages* (translated by A. Hamilton), Vol. V, Part I (London, 1897). *A History of Mediæval Political Theory in the West,* by R. W. and A. J. Carlyle (Vol. V, London, 1928), contains valuable chapters upon the political theory of the papacy in the thirteenth century, including a careful examination of the writings and deeds of Innocent III, but appeared too late, unfortunately, to be used in the preparation of the present volume.

For literature of general interest upon special topics in connection with the life and work of Innocent III the reader would do well to turn to the excellent manuals of J. W. Thompson (*Reference Studies in Medieval History,* Chicago, 1923), and L. J. Paetow (*Guide to the Study of Medieval History,* Berkeley, 1917). A new and revised edition of the latter is projected under the auspices of the Mediæval Academy of America.

SUPPLEMENTARY BIBLIOGRAPHY (1968)

A valuable selection of the letters of Innocent III has been translated and edited by C. R. Cheney and W. H. Semple, *Selected Letters of Innocent III Concerning England (1198-1216)* (Edinburgh, 1953). Biographies of Innocent III by L. Elliott-Binns (London, 1931), J. Clayton (Milwaukee, 1941) and Charles Smith (Baton Rouge, 1951), while each has merit, are disappointing for one reason or another. Good brief accounts of the pontificate of Innocent III may be found in the general textbooks of J. W. Thompson, *The Middle Ages,* 2 v. (New York, 1931), J. R. Strayer, *Western Europe in the Middle Ages* (New York, 1955) and in Carl Stephenson, *Mediaeval History,* 4th edition, revised and edited by Bryce Lyon (New York, 1962). There are valuable chapters in *The Cambridge Medieval History,* Vol. VI (London and New York, 1936), especially chapter i by E. F. Jacob, dealing with the whole career of Innocent III, and chapters xviii and xix, on political theories and on the doctrinal background of the Fourth Lateran Council, by W. H. V. Reade and A. H. Thompson, respectively. C. H. McIlwain, *The Growth of Political Thought in the West* (New York, 1932), Z. N. Brooke, *The English Church and the Papacy from the Conquest to the Reign of John* (Cambridge, 1931), Walter Ullmann, *The Growth of Papal Government in the Middle Ages,* 2nd edition (London, 1962) and Steven Runciman, *A History of the Crusades,* 3 v. (Cambridge, 1951-1954) are all of first-rate quality and are very helpful both for a fuller understanding of Innocent III and bibliographically. *The Later Crusades,* R. N. Wolff and H. R. Hazard, eds. (Philadelphia, 1961), the second volume in a projected five-volume cooperative *A History of the Crusades,* edited by K. M. Setton, has a good deal of material about Innocent III in connection with the Albigensian and Fourth Crusades.

Books on other special topics may be found in the bibliographies contained in the books listed above and in the 1931 edition of Paetow's *Guide,* reprinted without revision in 1959. J. L. LaMonte made a very successful attempt in the bibliographies in his *The World of the Middle Ages* (New York, 1949) to include primarily books which had appeared since 1931. For titles since 1949 one must turn to bibliographies in other books and to the pages of *Speculum,* the quarterly periodical published by The Medieval Academy of America. *Innocent III, Vicar of Christ or Lord of the World?* (Boston, 1963), edited by James E. Powell, contains excerpts on the problem indicated from some of the principal authorities both American and European: there is a helpful introduction and there are very useful suggestions for further reading.

INDEX

111